"Now tell us all about the war,
And what they fought each other for."
Robert Southey

The Battle of Waterloo

In the same series

The Battle of Fontenoy
The Battle of Salamis

Background Books for Wargamers and Modellers

The Battle of Waterloo
B. J. Hurren

William Luscombe

First published in Great Britain by
William Luscombe Publisher Ltd
The Mitchell Beazley Group,
Artists House,
14–15 Manette Street,
London, W1V 5LB
1975

© 1975 by B. J. Hurren

All Rights Reserved. No part of this publication
may be reproduced, stored in a retrieval system,
or transmitted, in any form or by any means,
electronic, mechanical, photocopying, recording or
otherwise, without the prior permission of the
Copyright owner

ISBN 0 86002 057 6

Phototypeset by Tradespools Ltd, Frome, Somerset
Printed in Great Britain by
Tinling (1973) Limited, Prescot, Merseyside

Acknowledgement

The author's grateful thanks are due to Macmillan London and Basingstoke and St. Martin's Press for their kind permission to reproduce on pages 52–53, extracts from *Europe Against Napoleon* by Anthony Brett-James.

Contents

1 The Road to Waterloo *11*
2 Two Points of View *19*
3 The Opponents *32*
4 Battlefield Tactics *41*
5 Sinews of War *52*
6 Among Those Present... *63*
7 Order of Battle *71*
8 Terrain and Weather *85*
9 Preliminary Moves *94*
10 Quatre Bras and Ligny *104*
11 Let Battle Commence *117*
12 The Gamble that Failed *127*
13 At the End of the Day *138*
14 Assessing the Battle *147*
15 Waterloo as a Wargame *156*
16 Aftermath *165*
Recommended reading *172*
Index *175*

Illustrations

Plates (between pages 24 and 25 and 56 and 57)
1 Napoleon
2 Wellington
3 19th Century map of the battlefields of Quatre Bras and Waterloo
4 Sir Thomas Lawrence's superb portrait of the Duke of Wellington
5 The Earl of Uxbridge orders the cavalry forward
6 The 92nd Foot charge with the Scots Greys
7 The charge of the French Heavy cavalry
8 Marshal Ney
9 Marshal Soult
10 Lt.-General Sir Thomas Picton, G.C.B.
11 View from Mont St. Jean at the commencement of the final allied charge
12 The meeting of Wellington and Blücher after the battle
13 Feldmarschall Gebhard Leberecht von Blücher

Acknowledgements to Plates

Plate 4 is reproduced by Gracious permission of Her Majesty the Queen. Plate 7 is the Copyright of Wellington Museum, Apsley House, and is reproduced with their kind permission. The remaining illustrations are all from the Mansell Collection whose help and permission to reproduce are gratefully acknowledged.

Diagrams and Maps
1 The alternatives facing Napoleon *22*
2 Map illustrating Wellington's dilemma *26*
3 The tactics employed at Waterloo *48–49*
4 Wellington's view of the battlefield *88*
5 How Napoleon saw the battlefield *92*
6 General dispositions of the Allied, Prussian and French armies during the battle *119*

Diagrams and maps by Chris Evans

I
The Road to Waterloo

The grass roots of the decisive battle of 18th June, 1815, near the village of Waterloo, are to be found in the apparently trivial fact that the first territorial prize to fall to the French Revolutionaries was Belgium which became united to France in 1795. That event was to influence Napoleon's decision as to where he should fight what turned out to be his final action.

Napoleon never actually met Wellington, though the two Commanders could see each other by telescope across the valley of their military confrontation at Mont Saint Jean, to the South of Brussels by the present N.5 motorway. Wellington had, however, repeatedly defeated individual marshals of the French army; and the long trail of his successes should have warned Napoleon that he was taking on a military commander of far greater stature than his derisory term of 'Sepoy General' indicated.

Born in 1769 (the same year as Napoleon), Arthur Wellesley, the fourth son of the 1st Earl of Mornington, had notched up considerable military experience abroad by the time he was promoted Lieutenant-General (25th April, 1808). A good starting point for this narrative is April, 1809, when, as Sir Arthur Wellesley, he was given command in Portugal after the retreat and death of Sir John Moore at Corunna (1809). He swiftly made his mark against the French in the Iberian Peninsula, defeating the forces under Marshal Nicolas Soult at Oporto on 12th May.

He then crossed into Spain, and, reinforced by the Spanish army, resoundingly defeated Marshal Claude Perrin Victor and General Horace Sebastiani de la Porta, at Talavera de la Reina (Central Spain). In reward for these victories he was created Viscount Wellington in 1809 (the name comes from a village near the original family home in Somerset).

Meanwhile, faraway in Central Europe, Napoleon had totally defeated the forces of the Archduke Charles of Austria in a great battle on 5th/6th July, 1809, at Wagram, a village near Vienna. Angered by the British commander's success in Spain, Napoleon then appointed Marshal André Massena as supremo of considerably augmented French forces in the Peninsula. This increase in enemy strength obliged Wellington to withdraw – to plan and in good order – before the numerically far superior army of Marshal Soult, at Almeida, 27th August, 1810. Exactly a month later, he repulsed an advance directed by Marshal Massena at Busaco (Buzaco), and then retired behind fortified and prepared lines of defences in the Torres Vedras area, to the north of, and defending the approaches to, Lisbon.

Marshal Massena found Wellington's position impregnable, and, with supplies running short, he ordered a contraction of the lines of communication and supply, thus giving Wellington the chance for harrying actions. In fact, the French withdrew to Salamanca whilst Wellington (now with the full confidence of Parliament in England) was ordered to go over to the offensive. There followed defeat of the French at Fuentes de Onoro, and Albuera, with Almeida re-taken (16th May,

1811). The next target was Badajoz, but this, for the time being, proved too much of a strong-point.

So Wellington switched the offensive to Ciudad Rodrigo which, in a brilliantly executed action, was taken on 19th January, 1812. For this success he was acclaimed in England and created Earl Wellington, whilst the Spanish made him Duke of Ciudad Rodrigo.

The next objective was Badajoz, which, as earlier, proved a tough nut to crack. It was invested on 16th March, 1812, but not captured until 6th April – and then only after heavy casualties.

Ignoring the string of defeats in Iberia, Napoleon had his eyes turned east, and on 22nd June, 1812, declared war on Russia. As the Grande Armée moved eastwards, so Wellington moved nearer to France, and on 22nd July inflicted a crushing defeat on the army of Marshal Marmont at Salamanca. This was as a stepping stone to Valladolid, whilst Wellington himself entered Madrid on 12th August. Honours were showered on him: he was raised to Marquess and made Generalissimo of the Spanish Armies in September. In the first week of that month Napoleon had fought the indecisive battle at Borodino, and had moved on to Moscow.

In a curious parallel, just as Napoleon began the retreat from Moscow (18th October) so Wellington realised he had overstretched his strength, for faced with the concentrated Division of General Bertrand Clausel at Burgos he decided to withdraw, hurriedly, right back to Ciudad Rodrigo (21st October). Winter had set in for Napoleon and Wellington in their widely separated campaigns.

In March, 1813, emboldened by the tragedy of the Grande Armée in Russia, Austria, Prussia and Russia formed an alliance against France. And, in a fresh eruption of what Napoleon viewed as 'The Spanish Ulcer', the offensive was re-opened on 22nd May, 1813, when Wellington's armies crossed the Portuguese frontier into Spain. Two forces moved eastwards, the columns meeting at Toro (4th June). The French abandoned the great city of Burgos; and, in pursuit, Wellington fought and won a devastating battle at Vitoria. There on 21st June, 1813, Napoleon's brother, Joseph Bonaparte (King of Spain) with Marshal Jean-Baptiste Jourdan, was routed with staggering losses, the French retreating across the Pyrénees into France. For this superb action, Wellington was promoted Field Marshal. However, there were pockets of French forces still in Spain.

In the closing days of August, Napoleon inflicted a heavy defeat on the allied army at Dresden (26th/27th August) whilst Wellington advanced on San Sebastian which suffered a terrific bombardment (31st August) and surrendered on 9th September, an action followed up by the British army crossing into France on 7th October, 1813. This year ended on the Spanish/French front with the French driven back to defence at Bayonne after defeats at the battles of the Nivelle (16th November) and Nive (9th/13th December). Whilst that operation was proceeding steadily, in Central Europe the allies inflicted an overwhelming defeat on Napoleon at Leipzig (16th–19th October). Here, in scenes of shocking carnage, the French force of 160,000 was overwhelmed by the allied 240,000, and more than 40,000 French soldiers were killed.

The immediate consequence of Leipzig was that the House of Orange was restored in Holland (17th November, 1813) and Belgium annexed from France to its dominion. This was followed (6th December) with the proclamation of the Prince of Orange as sovereign of the United Netherlands.

Wellington continued the pressure in S.W. France, with a blockade of Bayonne, sealing up the French defence there with two detached divisions, whilst chasing Marshal Soult to defeat at the battle of Orthez (27th February, 1814).

A week later, allied pressure increased towards Paris, with Marshals Victor and Ney fighting delaying actions. A fierce combat at Laon ended with French forces surrendering to the Prussian army (9th/10th March), and the road to Paris – only 80 miles distant – was open. In fact, the city of Paris surrendered (30th March), and negotiations with the allies for the abdication of Napoleon opened on 5th April. On 11th the Emperor formally abdicated. Even as that was taking place, after a number of minor actions Wellington fought and again defeated Marshal Soult in the battle of Toulouse (10th April). Two days later, with the British army occupying Toulouse, Wellington heard of the abdication. The convention by which hostilities formally ceased was signed on 18th April.

Wellington was summoned to Paris, where his command of the French language was invaluable in negotiation, and almost at once despatched to Madrid to sort out a ticklish political problem. Thus he did not reach England until 23rd May. A triumphal homecoming was crowned by his elevation to a dukedom, and he received countless honours and gifts. But there was to be no respite. Louis XVIII had returned to Paris, 3rd May; and Napoleon had been taken to Elba, 4th May. The Treaty of Paris (30th May) imposed easy terms on the French, and re-settlement of Europe was passed to the charge of a congress of nations in Vienna.

In a curious appointment, the new Duke of Wellington was made H.B.M. Ambassador in Paris (5th July, 1814); but in this rôle he did not shine, so that after some controversy and friction he left in February, 1815, to take over the chair of senior British plenipotentiary at the Congress of Vienna.

Events then took a startling turn. Napoleon escaped from confinement at Elba (between Corsica and the Italian mainland) and landed on 26th February, 1815, at Fréjus, near Cannes, on the French Riviera. He then headed for Paris which he reached on 20th March.

In Vienna, to a background of gaiety and intrigue, monarchs and ministers had for months been arguing about the political pattern and boundaries of the New Europe which, realistically, was in style and shape no more than a restoration of the pre-Revolution formulae. Fortunately, with all the wrangling over the share-out of the rich cake, nothing had been decided beyond, in principle, a restoration of the monarchy and a revived aristocracy in France. When, in the first week of March, Napoleon's return to France became known, and further that he was, with great public acclaim, heading for Paris, Congress was stung to action by the imperial bee, and forthwith proclaimed Napoleon outlawed, set aside its casual considerations, and immediately organised a military alliance against him – that is, against Napoleon personally rather than France – and all this in less than a fortnight.

Thus a Europe sick of decades of war was swiftly bonded together against the prime cause of a new interruption to Peace. Every diplomatic ploy was thereby closed to a France headed by Napoleon; and had the battle of Waterloo been won on the field by the French it would have availed nothing, because all Europe would have remained united against Napoleon and determined to overthrow him as soon as possible.

In fact, despite the plaudits of the Paris mob, Napoleon was in a desperate position, not least because much of France (and even some of his own generals) was against renewal of war. To rally all the French behind his standard his best gamble lay in recovery of Belgium, which had been the first prize to be captured by revolutionary France, and the first to be taken from her by the gentlemen in Vienna. Napoleon clearly saw the advantages of action against the allies in Belgium; and he decided, rightly, that his only hope of full and accepted re-establishment, symbolically and militarily, lay in the capture of Brussels.

The clash at Waterloo thus represented a head-on collision between the one State of the dynamic Revolutionaries and Republicans against the several States of the die-hard Dynasts. Indeed, that formula extended to the commanders themselves, with Napoleon self-appointed Commander-in-Chief and Wellington nominated on 28th March by the allies as Commander of the Anglo-Netherland and Hanoverian forces in Europe (distinct from the Prussian army commanded by Field Marshal Blücher, and the armies of Austria and Russia, distant from the focal point of Brussels).

Brief reminders

Since anyone can have a blind spot, no apology is offered for emphasising here some points which are obvious but which, if thoughtlessly overlooked, could alter many aspects of the Waterloo wargame.

First, the importance of roads. The key factor here is not concerned with infantry or cavalry but with artillery. A light field battery could be taken easily across country, but the heavyweights preferred to have hard tracks or roads to get as near as possible to the scene of action. Only to a slightly less degree does that factor apply to the ammunition and supply wagons which, fully loaded, could be as heavy as big guns.

Secondly, speed of movement is an important factor. The fastest passage of a message was the speed of the bearer's horse. It is true that a race-horse can move at about 43 m.p.h. mounted, but the animals conveying the messages which meant so much in the battle of Waterloo and its run-in were military animals often going cross-country over considerable distances (and sometimes in the dark). Hence it would be realistic to consider 12–15 m.p.h. as transit speed for a messenger, and 10–12 m.p.h. for a coach with four horses, as maxima. For a full-equipped column on the move $3\frac{1}{2}$ m.p.h. is a top speed for infantry. The rate of progress can be gauged from the fact that the Imperial Guard left Paris 8th June and had moved 125 miles (205 km.) on 13th June.

Thirdly, the first railways did not come anywhere in Europe until long after Waterloo. There was a small canal system in France and Belgium, in the 17th and 18th Centuries, but there was nothing like the present network of waterways. Likewise, of course, for motorways. Thus any modern map should be used with the knowledge that in the early 19th Century things were much more simple. Incidentally, the first steam-boats between Dover and Calais date back to 1821.

2
Two Points of View
◆◆◆◆

The principal clause in the agreement the allies (Britain, Prussia, Austria and Russia) made on 25th March, 1815, was that each would have in the field 150,000 men until Napoleon was finally overthrown.

The grand strategy was quite simply to overwhelm Napoleon by having the enormous collective total of 795,000 men on the French frontiers, and they were to march on Paris by different yet converging routes.

This was fine in theory, but, for practical purposes, inclined to be 'pie in the sky'. The reality of the situation is revealed in the summarised figures that follow:

In quick time after his return to Paris, Napoleon assessed the French army to muster *in toto* 160,000 troops, all categories. But, on his abdication in 1814, conscription to service had been abolished, and so the army was diminishing daily. However, by an emotive appeal to patriotism, even blatant chauvinism, Napoleon lured back to the colours in just under two months no fewer than 80,000 veterans. By introducing again obligatory service he would have, in the autumn, some 500,000 men in arms.

Could he afford to wait that long – knowing that each week increased the strength of the allies against him? Weighing the pros and cons, the answer was in the negative. More than that, on 27th April he decided to attack before the Austrian and the Russian armies could reach the Rhine.

In one regard his military aim was simplified and clarified: his opposing commander was Wellington – he was *the* person to be defeated in the field. There would be tremendous kudos to be gained by victory over the victor of Spain, against whom so many of his marshals had failed. And, of course, there were old scores to settle with England, with 'perfidious Albion' against whom his invasion plans had come to nought in 1805 when Nelson destroyed the combined French and Spanish navies at Trafalgar.

The symbol, almost trade-mark, of Napoleon was the golden bee, a *motif* which appeared, for example, on imperial furnishings in the Louvre and elsewhere. And as a very busy bee he prepared for one of his famous concentrations of force that, almost without exception, took the enemy unawares.

So, on 3rd June he issued orders for just such a surprise concentration with which he expected to catch Wellington on the wrong foot, or at least guessing the wrong way. And since Wellington was stuck at Brussels as he tried to bring together his polyglot forces, then the capital of Belgium would be the principal objective.

The disposition of the available forces of the *Armée du Nord* on 3rd June was in this pattern: in general there were corps formations on a line from Lille to Strasbourg, major towns 240 miles apart. That was the N.E. 'front'. It was, as it were, facing Brussels, and there was a chain of connecting roads orientated N.W./S.E. which would permit, from Lille and from Metz, a rapid concentration at the centre of the front, by Charleroi.

From his Operations Room in Paris, Napoleon could see (from Lille to Metz) the 1st Corps commanded by

Count d'Erlon near Lille; then the 2nd Corps under Count Reille, based on Valenciennes; next the 3rd Corps led by Count Vandamme, at Mezières, just S.W. of Charleville, on the left bank of the Meuse; and 75 miles (120 km.) further S.E. the 4th Corps under Count Gerard, at Metz.

Behind this forward screen, Count Lobau had the 6th Corps, based on Laon.

Between the R. Aisne and the R. Sambre the veteran Marshal Grouchy had four corps of reserve cavalry.

The Imperial Guard was at Paris.

Far away to the right of the front, at Strasbourg on the Rhine, was the 5th Corps under Count Rapp.

There now took place one of those superb manoeuvres for which Napoleon had an enviable reputation. Ostentatiously showing himself in Paris, the Emperor caused a rapid concentration and contraction of the N.E. front so that a force of 124,000 men became positioned in a compact area S.W. of Charleroi, on French soil, embracing the small towns of Philippville-Beaumont-Solre sur Sambre.

The R. Sambre is important in this narrative. It is 110 miles (177 km.) long, rising near Avesnes-sur-Helpe, and flowing through Mauberge, then Charleroi, to Namur, as a tributary of the Meuse.

The Imperial Guard meanwhile left Paris on 8th June, and reached Avesnes on 13th June. Avesnes is 125 miles (205 km.) from Paris, and the diagram map shows that Napoleon could still exercise several options as to his ultimate approach to Brussels.

It was on the 14th June, at Avesnes, that Napoleon showed himself to his troops after a fast dash from Paris, and from that place addressed his first communiqué, to which reference will be made later.

The thing to note from the diagram map (Fig. 1, page 22) is that superficially the most favourable route to Brussels is via Mons. This was the opinion at which Wellington (and his staff) arrived as messages of French movements reached the capital.

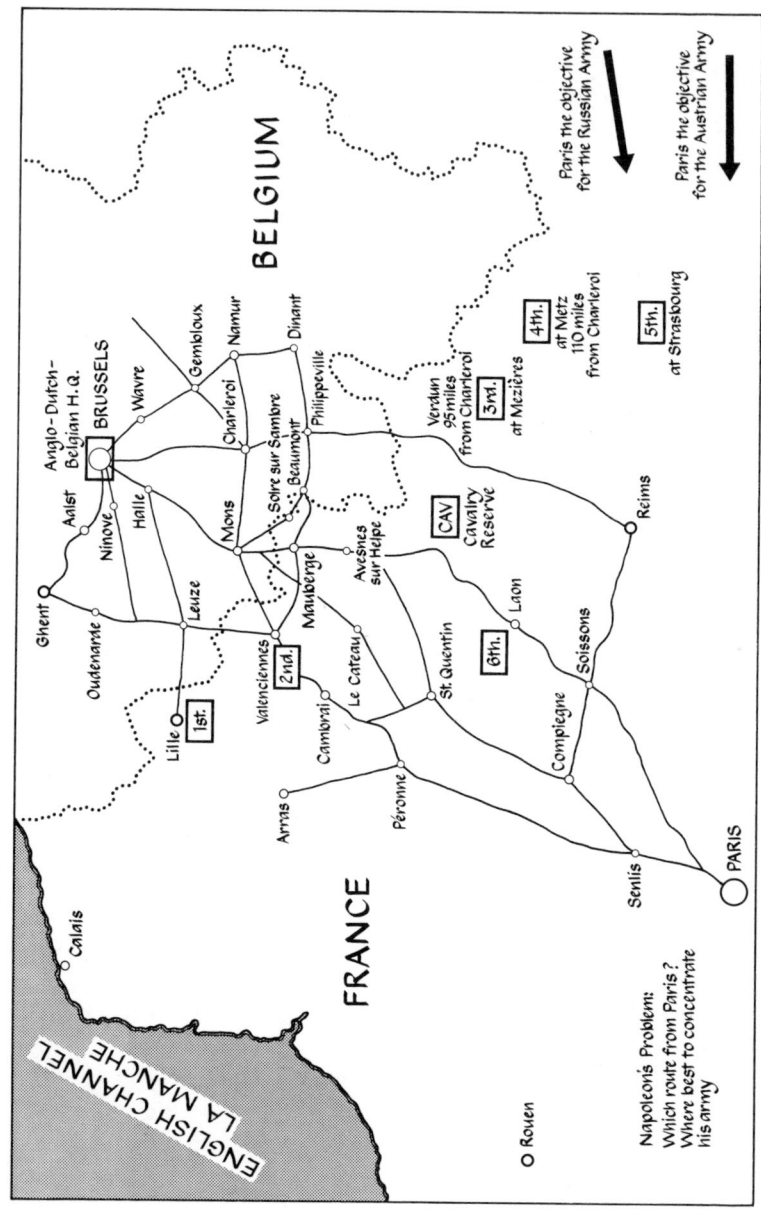

Fig. 1. This map illustrates the alternatives facing Napoleon as he made his last desperate challenge for the control of Europe.

But, still in Napoleon's chair, the position for options was, in summary form:

1. Napoleon calculated he had a maximum of 124,000 men, and this, considering the high proportion of cavalry and artillery, could
    (a) beat the Anglo-Dutch-Belgian force under Wellington at Brussels;
    (b) beat the Prussians based at Namur;
    (c) would not beat the combined (a) and (b) enemy forces in one action.
2. It would be possible, with great effort, to take on Wellington and immediately after engage the Prussians, or *vice versa*, in effect fighting two battles, one immediately after the other.
3. The best result would arise from beating either Wellington's forces or the Prussian forces, separated one from the other, and then make a diplomatic ploy to negotiate for whichever army had not been defeated in the field to come to terms and surrender without a fight.

That had been the position just before he left Paris for a dash to Avesnes; but now, as at 14th June, Napoleon saw the picture in far more roseate colours. There had been no link-up between Wellington and the Prussians, and it was almost elementary that he should take on and thrash the Prussians near Charleroi before turning on Wellington who was considerably to the North, in Brussels.

There was, of course, a *morale* factor in engaging the Prussians first. On 14th October, 1806, Napoleon with his Marshal Davout had fought two battles on the same day, with Prussian armies being defeated by Napoleon at Jena and by Davout at Auerstadt. And on 14th June, 1807, Napoleon had defeated the Prussians and Russians at Friedland, which had led to the Peace of Tilsit whereby Prussia lost half her territory. The French army led by Napoleon must therefore have been a bogey force to those Prussians with memories of such bloody defeats. Not surprisingly, then, Napoleon played on that angle in boosting the *morale* of his own troops; and in the very opening sentence of his address to his army from Avesnes he says: 'Soldiers! This day is the anniversary of Marengo and Friedland, which twice decided the destiny of Europe . . .'

Now to review the picture as seen by Wellington in Brussels.

The position, to a lesser man, could have seemed daunting, especially as it was Wellington himself who gave the opinion that the *morale* effect of the presence of Napoleon was as good as 40,000 troops (a statement which he qualified, later, by insisting that he did not mean 40,000 actual men on a battlefield).

Wellington's ace, which was not even up his sleeve, was that he could afford to wait, and Napoleon could not.

Furthermore, with a record of sensationally swift movements of troops, some such a manoeuvre could be expected from the Frenchman, viewed as an old dog who could not learn new tricks.

Hence, in principle it would be Napoleon chasing Wellington and not *vice versa*. Hence the basic assumption of a stand-still based on Brussels, on familiar ground, with all the lines of supply and communication safely secured.

Thus, though it was certain that Napoleon would come, the big question was *by which route?*

Although the term was not known in 1815, Wellington used the art of psychology in his appreciation of what his enemy would do. For himself, he was in Brussels, a city he knew well because after Eton, which he left in 1784 aged 15, he had had a private education under Maître Louis Goubert, a barrister resident in the capital. Yet, realistically, he was C. in C. of a very mixed and almost scratch army of British, Dutch, Belgians and Hanoverians, to a grand total of fewer than 100,000, with less than 75,000 of them in the actual Brussels area. Of that latter figure, under 25,000 were from Britain,

Plates 1 and 2 The two great commanders who fought each other for the first and only time at Waterloo: Napoleon (top) and Wellington

Plate 3 A 19th Century map based on contemporary sources, showing the battlefields of Quatre Bras and Waterloo in relation to Brussels and the French line of advance. For wargamers it provides a valuable indication of the roads available for the movement of artillery and heavy wagons

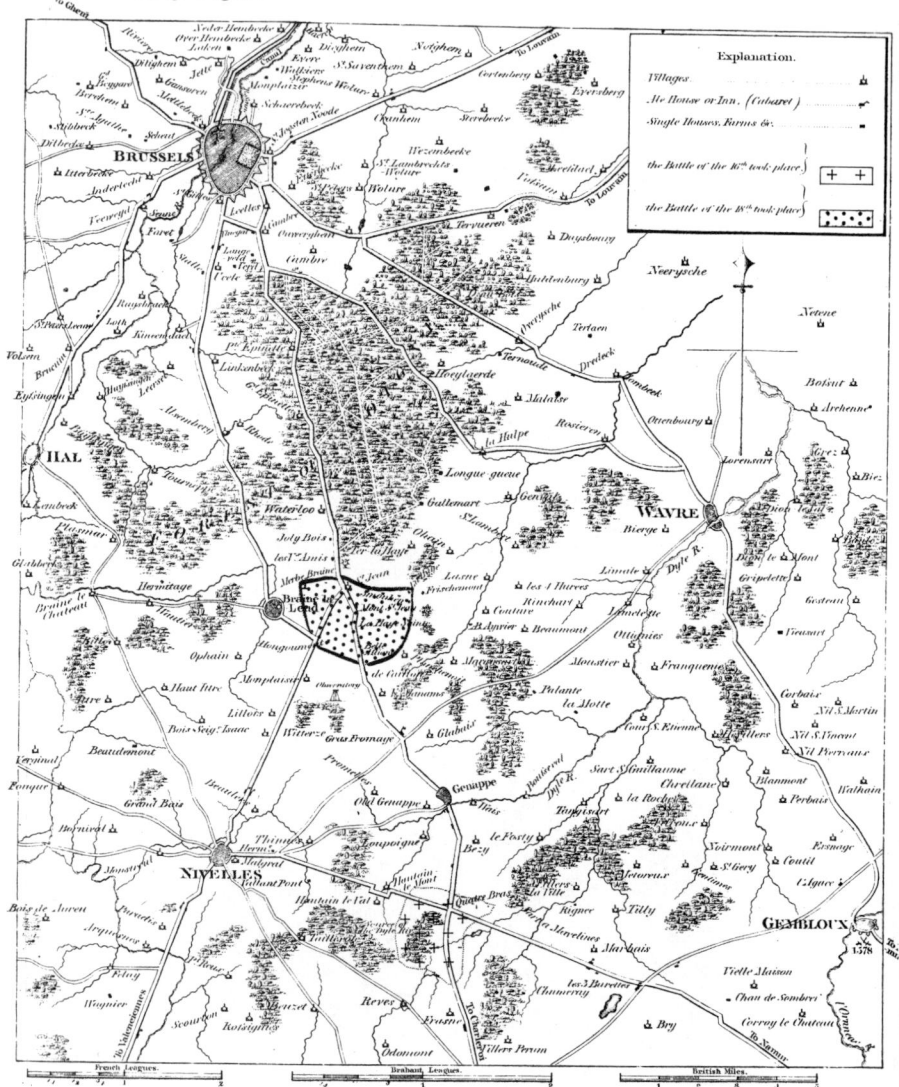

Plate 4 Sir Thomas Lawrence's superb portrait of Arthur Wellesley, Duke of Wellington. Reproduced by Gracious permission of Her Majesty the Queen

Plates 5 and 6 *These two engravings by George Jones of incidents from the battle are from a series published in 1816, and are probably as near as one can get to contemporary illustrations.* Top: *The Earl of Uxbridge ordering the cavalry forward at a critical moment in the battle.* Below: *the 92nd Foot and the Scots Greys together charge a demoralised French column*

and even of that figure a high proportion was of raw recruits, not yet battle-blooded.

In sheer numbers, Napoleon could overwhelm him. Scanning the muster rolls the consolidated totals gave him:

    31,253 British
    29,214 Netherlands Dutch and Belgians
    15,935 Hanoverians
     6,808 Brunswickers
     6,387 George III German Legion
     2,500 Nassau

Add in sundry auxiliaries, with supply and non-combatant medicos and contractors, and his command grossed 93,717 men.

However, there was the arrangement made with Feldmarschall Gebhard Leberecht von Blücher in May that if either were attacked by the French then the other would come to his aid – and Blücher had four Corps on Belgian soil.

Brussels was the key to the whole situation. If Brussels fell the Belgians of Flanders would throw in their hands, and the Dutch from the northern Netherlands would at best be cornered.

If Wellington could impose delaying actions, reinforcements could reach him by sea from England. From that angle, perhaps Napoleon would make for the N.E. coast of France, and on the Ghent–Bruges–Ostend sector cut communications with Britain. But that, Wellington decided, was not likely since it would leave Paris uncovered.

As Fig. 2 (page 26) shows, Brussels was the prize and every sign indicated that Napoleon would make a dead set for that target.

By which route would he come from Paris?

The most direct route was: Paris–Senlis–Cambrai–Valenciennes–Mons–Halle–Brussels.

As second choice: Paris–Soissons–Laon–Vervins–Mons.

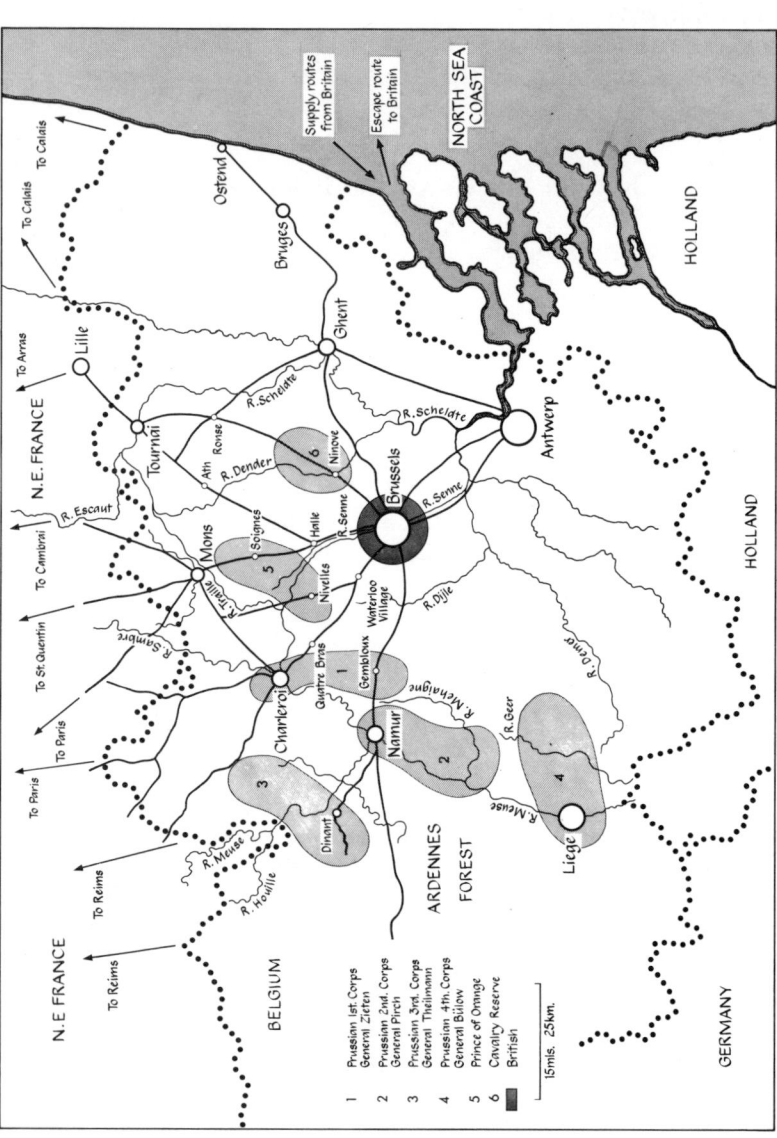

Fig. 2. Wellington's dilemma. Napoleon is with most of the Imperial Guard in Paris. Which route will he take to join battle with the Allies? Assuming Brussels to be the prime political target, then the most direct road is via Mons. However, Napoleon might favour first crushing the Prussians, in which case he would head for Charleroi. Or he might instead sneak through N.E. France and dying for Antwerp and the chance of cutting Wellington's line of

Supposing there was a need to avoid Mons, the best route could be Paris–Cambrai (through Senlis)–Valenciennes–cross northwards to Leuze–Ath–Halle and then on the Mons road to Brussels. There was in fact an alternative to Cambrai via St. Quentin – and if at St. Quentin, there was a chance to switch on to a right fork to Mons.

Finally, if on the Vervins–Mons road (the modern N.2), there could be a fork right to Avesnes to Charleroi, or perhaps a fork right by Mauberge to make an approach to Brussels on the direct route from the South (the modern N.5).

Musing on these options, Wellington would presumably organise the posting of spies on the various routes along which Napoleon, with the Imperial Guard, would have to travel.

At the same time, the French had perhaps as many as 150,000 troops spread out over the general line Lille–Strasbourg. Napoleon had the advantage of choosing the point at which he would order a concentration; but, except for bizarre and quite unpredictable reasons, the concentration would not be at the extremities but in the centre, that is to say, somewhere in the area of Mons.

What could Napoleon expect from his force of between 115,000 and 150,000 troops?

Thinking on almost exactly the same lines as his adversary, Wellington came to the conclusion that:

1. Napoleon would have an even-odds fight if he took on the Anglo-Dutch-German force plus the Prussians.
2. He would therefore try to take on one, and then the other.
3. His prime objective was to occupy Brussels.
4. He would head for Brussels with the minimum of delay.
5. He would concentrate his forces close to the direct line between Paris and Brussels, and Mons was the key town on that line.

In accord with that appreciation of the situation,

Wellington considered the disposition of his forces. In summary form, as shown on Fig. 2, he had:

1. The main body of the English army in and around Brussels.
2. The cavalry reserve (under Lord Uxbridge) west of Brussels, centred on Ninove on the R. Dender.
3. On the S.W. sector, astride the road to Mons, was the Netherlands Corps commanded by the Prince of Orange, in a kidney-shaped dispositional zone bounded by Enghien–Genappe–Quatre Bras–Frasnes–Mons.
4. Contingent with the left of Orange was the Prussian right, under General Zieten, astride the route Marcinelle–Charleroi–Gembloux, on the left bank zone of the R. Sambre.
5. The remaining part of the S.E. sector was covered by the Prussians, under the overall command of Blücher, who was with the Prussian 2nd Corps based on Namur. The 3rd Corps was centred on Dinant, and the 4th Corps on Liège.

Wellington could regard the disposition of his forces with some satisfaction, for if, as he was self-convinced, Napoleon advanced on Mons then the Corps commanded by the Prince of Orange would fight like the devil in the knowledge that the main British army was behind them, the main British cavalry reserve was on their right, and the crack Prussian Corps under Zieten positioned on their left.

Why was Wellington so sure the enemy would come via Mons? Because that was the route of open country, with room to manoeuvre his massive army.

But if, by chance, Napoleon elected to come in via Charleroi, then firstly, he would again have powerful armies on both flanks before meeting the main body of the British. Secondly, on the Charleroi road after Quatre Bras and Genappe, the enemy would be deprived of the ability to manoeuvre by the Forest of Soignes.

Thus, in this great ballet of manoeuvre, the corps were taking up positions for the Curtain Up – which we may set as being the evening of Tuesday, 13th June, when vigilant outposts of General Zieten's 1st Corps spotted unusual night activity in the direction of Beaumont, 16 miles (25 km.) S.W. of Charleroi. There appeared to be numerous bivouac fires; but as Beaumont was in France, across the Belgian frontier line, there was not necessarily any cause for alarm.

The wargamer should now pause to take note that the first of numerous delays in communication took place. It is easy to understand with hindsight what happened, and even why; but to introduce realism it is necessary to emphasise that intelligence of this undue activity in the night at Beaumont – which would today be flashed in seconds by radio or telephone – was conveyed, in strict military escalation, from the foremost observer to his immediate superior, thence at least 10 miles to Charleroi, thence on to General Zieten's H.Q. between Gembloux and the R. Sambre, a further 12 miles. In his turn, Zieten had to transmit the information to the Command H.Q. of Blücher at Namur, 8 miles further S.E., and then Blücher had to assess the value of the intelligence and act accordingly. In fact, his action was entirely correct: he received the message late on Wednesday, 14th June, and without delay despatched orders for:

1. Zieten to make a careful tactical withdrawal N.E. towards Charleroi, and then, in good time, with delaying tactics against any enemy advance, to withdraw steadily back, still N.E. along the road through Gilly, Fleurus, and Ligny, to link up with the main body of the Prussian army which was being concentrated on Sombreffe.

2. At the same time Blücher ordered the 2nd, 3rd and 4th Prussian Corps to converge on Sombreffe. (Note: all these villages are on the modern N.21 road linking Gembloux–Charleroi.)

3. A message detailing these projected movements was despatched at once to Wellington in Brussels, 35 miles distant and to the N.W. of Namur. This message was sent by the safe hand of a Prussian officer who had started from Zieten's command post; and it was not

until 3 o'clock (15.00 hours) on the afternoon of Thursday, 15th June that Wellington received that message.

Fortunately, provision for full liaison had been made well in advance, for on Wellington's staff, in the closest contact, was General the Baron von Müffling as Blücher's personal representative. With this alert in hand the Baron urgently contacted the Duke; and after reading out Blücher's message he asked the English commander whether he might send back the Prussian officer courier with information as to where the Anglo-Netherland-German forces would now be ordered to concentrate, because in his understanding of his Feldmarschall's thinking, the Prussian army would by now have mainly concentrated on Sombreffe and would have prepared advance lines at the village of Ligny.

Much later, in his memoirs, Baron Müffling revealed from his diary Notes exactly what the Duke replied. As translated by Colonel Sir Charles Yorke (1790–1880), who was himself with Wellington in Spain and at Waterloo, and who himself became a General in 1865, the pronouncement of the Duke was:

> 'If all is as General Zieten supposes, I will concentrate on my left wing, and so be in readiness to fight in conjunction with the Prussian army. Should, however, a portion of the enemy's forces come by Mons, I must concentrate more towards my centre. This is the reason I must wait for positive news from Mons before I fix the rendez-vous. Since, however, it is certain that the troops *must* march, though it is uncertain upon what precise spot they must march, I will order all to be in readiness, and will direct a brigade to move at once towards Quatre Bras.'

Shortly afterwards a further message came from Blücher to inform Baron Müffling that he was concentrating on Sombreffe. At once the Baron acquainted the Duke with the facts (that had now replaced surmises), and yet again Wellington declared that whilst the movements directed by the Feldmarschall were admirable he could still not resolve where the point of concentration would be until he had had definite intelligence from Mons.

3
The Opponents

Whilst from various sources Wellington received – or waited for – battle intelligence, the nature of the two leaders can be examined. It is important to appreciate that both men had the magic and rare quality of Leadership. Many capable commanders have imagined that they possessed this almost indefinable quality, and have failed because in fact they lacked it. But Napoleon and Wellington unquestionably could inspire men to seek (as Shakespeare puts it) the bubble reputation even in the cannon's mouth, or, as lesser men would say, to stand and fight as a disciplined army with confidence in its commander's generalship.

As the messages were winging from Zieten to Blücher to Müffling to Wellington, Napoleon was handing out the text of a pep-talk. He had reached Avesnes-sur-Helpe (modern route N.2) about 26 miles South of Brussels. With his army now grouped in a nucleus a few miles ahead, and still on French soil, he issued an Order of the Day dated 14th June, 1815, which began:

> Soldiers! This day is the anniversary of Marengo and of Friedland, which twice decided the destiny of

Europe. Then, as after Austerlitz, as after Wagram, we were too generous! We believed in the protestations and in the oaths of princes whom we left on their thrones. Now, leagued together, they aim at the independence and the most sacred rights of France. They have commenced the most unjust of aggressions. Let us march to meet them. Are they and we no longer the same men?

There was much more in that style; and, to be fair, the message makes better reading in its native French than in its translation which, in places, is faintly absurd. Nevertheless, after inveighing against the wicked allies the ending was:

Soldiers! We have forced marches to make, battles to fight, dangers to encounter! But, with firmness, Victory will be ours. The rights, the honour and the happiness of the country will be recovered! To every Frenchman who has a heart, the moment is now arrived to conquer or to die!

All that, of course, came just prior to the final eclipse of his fortunes, and to understand what really made Napoleon tick it is probably necessary to recall the elements of his beginnings – facts rarely mentioned in history books. Note particularly the change from 'Buonaparte' to 'Bonaparte'.

He was born at Ajaccio, Corsica, the fourth child of Carlo Buonaparte and Letizia Ramolino, a couple who in all had eight children surviving from 13 born. As with many of humble origin who rise to fame, the true family circumstances were later inflated by describing the father as a lawyer. Well there are lawyers and lawyers, and in the mid-18th Century in a primitive island whose inhabitants were described by Seneca as robbers, liars and atheists, Carlo was probably at best a court usher. Furthermore, when this Genoese dependency was ceded to France in 1768, when Napoleon was not even born, his father became what would later be termed a collaborator, working with the French. Legends about noble ancestry, even to links with the Buonaparte family of 12th Century Bologna, were scoffed at by Napoleon himself, for the fact is he was of humble origins and made his way in the world by his own qualities and character.

Because of feelings against the family, the father wangled his bright son into the French College at Autun (Burgundy) at age 9; he only stayed there 3 months, and then continued his education at the military college at Brienne-le-Château (25 miles (40 km.) East of Troyes, S.E. of Paris) where he stayed 5 years. He next moved to the military academy in Paris where, with worries about his impoverished family, he remained for one year, and in the final examinations was placed 42nd out of 51. His first posting was as a Lieutenant of Artillery (1785) at Valence. He applied himself diligently to military study, and was promoted Captain in 1792. A year later, in rebellion against the French rule the local Corsican leader* condemned the Buonaparte family to 'perpetual execration and infamy' and thus, shepherded by Napoleon, the family moved across to metropolitan France and from 1796 became Bonaparte.

The weather-cock fortunes of the political leaders of the Revolution gave Napoleon a series of chances. In 1793 he was graded *chef de bataillon* and became head of a brigade. After commanding artillery successfully against British troops at Toulon he was made a Brigadier General when the French re-captured the town. In February, 1794, he became commandant of artillery of the French army in Italy, but within months, with a new political upheaval in Paris, he was made unemployed and put on half-pay. Another change made him head of the Army of the Interior (1795); and then to the post he most coveted, C. in C. the army in Italy, which country he rapidly subdued. Following his abortive adventure in Egypt, which foundered on Nelson's victory at the Nile in 1798, Napoleon returned to Italy and a second campaign there which led to the victory he never forgot

*Paoli Pasquale, who himself died an exile in England in 1807.

– the great battle of Marengo (14th June, 1800), a village near Alessandria, Piedmont – it was at this battle that he wore the grey coat made familiar in so many paintings, and in which he was actually buried at St. Helena.

The long record of military successes thereafter becomes monotonous. What is almost invariably ignored, however, is that after the tremendous defeat of the French at Leipzig (16th–19th October, 1813) he fought a series of losing engagements against allied forces led by Prince von Schwartzenberg of Austria. The French lost 6,000 men in the battle at Craonne (7th March, 1814) and then Napoleon found himself outnumbered by two to one at Laon. Forced back by the allies, across the R. Seine and R. Aube, Schwartzenberg managed to bring in troops to outnumber Napoleon by three to one, and the French lost desperately at Arcis-sur-Aube on 21st March, 1814. Pompously declaring he would defend his country foot by foot, Napoleon withdrew westwards in Lorraine, and left his marshals, Marmont and Mortier, a bare 20,000 troops to defend Paris.

Thus, in coming to face Wellington the fallen Emperor had plenty of long-ago successes but numerous recent reverses in the running battles of 1814. He could bask in the glamour of ancient victories up to a point – but he badly needed a crushing success against Wellington to bolster up his toppled prestige.

Napoleon enjoyed a resilient temperament, but his political operations tended to dull his military genius. That genius rested almost entirely on an unerring eye for a weakness in the enemy in the field – he could spot that weakness, and exploit it almost before his opposing commander realised the opportunity given to Napoleon.

This had happened so many times in the past that it was difficult for his marshals not to continue to regard him as a wonder-boy and miracle worker. Bewitched by his darting mind, and conscious of their shortcomings before his military brilliance, the lowliest fusilier and the most experienced marshal alike feared to go contrary to his orders or even put up ideas of their own. He was a leader of men, but a feared leader – men followed him because they were afraid of their own assessments being so inferior to his. That point the wargamer could well exploit because, as is clearly shown in the dramatic actuality, Napoleon made a sequence of major blunders both in choice of men and in place of manoeuvre. It is thus a fact that Wellington was right in his expectation that Mons should have been the route of advance by the French. Had Napoleon come that way the whole scale and scope of the action would have been entirely different.

Next, a brief survey of Feldmarschall Gebhard Leberecht von Blücher who lived 1742–1819.

In the first place, he was 27 years older than both Napoleon and Wellington. It could be said that this man of indomitable spirit and superb personal courage was born at the wrong time, for though he loved the army and regarded it as his chosen career he had by force of circumstances to withdraw three times into civilian life before Waterloo.

He was born of a well-to-do professional family at Rostock (coast of modern East Germany but then in Prussia). At age 14 he enlisted in the Swedish cavalry against the wishes of his parents. In the Seven Years War (1756–63) he served as a hussar, and resigned when he was denied the promotion he deserved.

On the accession of Frederick William II, king of Prussia, in 1786, Blücher returned to the army, with the rank of major. In 1794 he was promoted major-general in command of the army of the Lower Rhine. And at the great battle of Jena (1806) which was a triumph for Napoleon, he fought a splendid rearguard action. Nevertheless, soon after Jena he was captured at Ratkau near Lübeck. His release came when he was exchanged for the French Marshal Victor, but Napoleon himself stipulated that Blücher should not rejoin the Prussian army. So, once again, he went into retirement, nursing a ferocious hatred of the French.

In the crisis year of 1813, and now aged 71, he returned to the army again, and fought with distinction at Lutzen (2nd May, 1813) and then Bautzen (20th May), both encounters being indecisive but definitely in favour of Napoleon. However on 26th August, 1813, at Katzbach, Blücher inflicted a resounding defeat on the French under Marshal Alexandre Macdonald. For that victory he was created Prince von Wahlstatt (the name of a neighbouring village).

In the summer of 1814 he once more retired from the army, to his estates, but with the return of Napoleon from exile in Elba he was yet again summoned to rejoin the army, now as C. in C. Prussian troops in Belgium, with General Neidhardt von Gneisenau as his Chief of Staff.

Feldmarschall von Blücher thus had a long-standing score to settle with Napoleon. Disparagingly described by his enemies as rough and ill-educated, Blücher nevertheless possessed furious energy, resilience, personal bravery and above all common sense. At Waterloo he was the only white-haired commander present, and yet his vigour surpassed that of men half his age. When he died at his castle at Kriblowitz in Silesia in 1819 he left behind a new tradition for the Prussian army – a regular General Staff to advise commanders.

The Duke of Wellington was born into the Anglo-Irish aristocracy. He is listed in many reference books as Arthur Wellesley, but the original family name was Colley, changed for legal reasons in 1728 to Wesley and yet again in 1798 to Wellesley, the medieval version of Wesley. The boy was the fourth son of the 1st Earl of Mornington and his wife Anne, who was the eldest daughter of Viscount Dungannon. In due course (1806), as Colonel of the 33rd Regiment of Foot, Arthur married the Hon. Catherine Pakenham, daughter of the 2nd Baron Longford.

Despite that excellent form in the aristocracy stakes, his career all along owed much to his brother, Richard

Colley Wellesley, who rose to become Governor-General of India (in the days before establishment of the office of Viceroy) and was in 1797 created (1) Baron Wellesley in the English peerage, and then (2) Marquis Wellesley in the Irish peerage.

It was this brother, as Lord Mornington, who in 1787 secured for the future Duke a commission in the 73rd Highland Regiment, as an Ensign aged 18. In a curious progression arising from the system of the times, the young officer moved through five different regiments until in 1793 he purchased a majority in the 33rd Foot (later renamed The Duke of Wellington's Regiment). And five months later, in the same regiment, he acquired the Lieutenant-Colonelcy.

His first battle action was at Boxtel, Bois-le-Duc, in Holland in 1794.

Then as a full Colonel he went to India in 1796. There, with his elder brother as Governor-General, he applied himself rigorously to the study of military sciences, abandoning (as one gossipy note put it) music and games of cards in order to concentrate on his work.

He left India in 1805, and, in the casual way of politics of that period, became M.P. for Rye (1806), Mitchell (1807) and Newport (1807–9) whilst still continuing his military career and being promoted Lieutenant-General, 1808.

The general details of his progress through the Peninsular War have already been discussed, but as a reminder, he was created a Field Marshal in 1813 after the defeat of Joseph Bonaparte's army at Vitoria.

This is perhaps an appropriate point to note that the Duke of Wellington finally carried no fewer than nine military marshals' batons. Of these, two were standard British, and one of gold especially made for presentation to him by the Prince Regent (later George IV); he was also:

Marshal-General, Portuguese Army;
Field-Marshal of Hanover;

Field-Marshal, Netherlands Army;
Field-Marshal, Austrian Army;
Field-Marshal, Prussian Army;
Captain-General, Spanish Army;
(and bearer of the marshal's staff of the High Constable of England).

Wellington was a direct contrast to the Man-of-the-People pose of Napoleon. A great deal of antipathy was generated by his political career subsequent to Waterloo, but that should not be allowed to dim his military genius. In this regard, he has been compared with Publius Cornelius Scipio, the famous general of the Second Punic War of Ancient Rome. For 16 years Napoleon strove against England – for 17 years Hannibal fought against Rome. The ancient struggle ended at Zama, and the English triumphed at Waterloo. Scipio and Wellington both held for several years high command in distant campaigns. In Spain, Scipio, as with Wellington, successively encountered and overthrew almost all the top-rating generals of the enemy before taking on the chief commander. Both Scipio and Wellington restored confidence after a succession of reverses. And both closed a prolonged, perilous, war by a crushing defeat that debarred all hope of a recovery both by the vanquished commander and the troops under his command.

Wellington could be a difficult man to deal with. He had his measure of aristocratic pride, and though never admitting it, adhered to this code for dealing with his social inferiors: 'Be mean, but keep them keen.' He could be haughty, taciturn, uncommunicative, secretive, and possessed an Irish turn of phrase that could reveal a streak of gay insouciance, or equally well deliver a verbal haymaker. Above all, in his military career, he knew how to wait – and that was a quality Napoleon never acquired.

After several hours of waiting, with Baron Müffling on tenterhooks, a message as to the situation at Mons was delivered to Wellington in Brussels around midnight, 15th June. Without delay the Duke proceeded to call on Baron Müffling to acquaint him with the fact that his intelligence was that no French troops were advancing on the Mons sector, and that the mass of Napoleon's force was undoubtedly committed to the Charleroi area. Consequently, he had the honour to inform the Prussian liaison officer that he had given the order for British troops to advance upon the key crossroads called Quatre Bras. However, he added – with the coolness which was known on the Continent as *sang froid habituel* – that for the moment he himself would not actually be accompanying the troops because he had an obligation to remain at the ball being given that night – it was now well into Friday – by the Duchess of Richmond.

The news the Duke received was far behind events. In fact, at 3 a.m. (03.00 hours) on the Thursday morning, 15th June, the French had crossed the Belgian frontier, and in three huge columns were marching N.E. towards Charleroi, keeping to the right bank of the R. Sambre.

And at 07.00 hours that same morning, the French General Louis Auguste Bourmont, commanding the 14th Infantry Division, quit his troops, crossed unmolested to the Prussian corps under Zieten, and revealed all that he knew of the strength of the French army and the plan of Napoleon for its combat deployment.

The action was just beginning. Before any major clash occurs, however, it could be useful to examine the battle methods favoured by the opponents.

4
Battlefield Tactics

It is impossible not to feel admiration for Wellington in his brilliant appreciation of the tactics which his adversary would use, and the scheme evolved to frustrate them without any suspicion arising in Napoleon's mind of the trap into which he was being lured. It has to be remembered that in almost every stage of the fighting Napoleon had available, more or less on the spot, great numerical superiority over his opponents – and he was hoodwinked into not exploiting the fact.

On the other hand, the position of Napoleon, and his thinking, may perhaps be best illustrated by facts from World War II when an immensely successful and highly competent German Army was defeated by Soviet troops inferior in equipment, training and battle experience. In the show-down of 1941, the German attack on Russia was launched with the assumption that 1 German would equate with 14 Russians (for such was the poor opinion held by the German High Command of the opposition on their eastern front). In the event, in the fighting through 1941 and 1942, in the grand totals the numerical odds were $17\frac{1}{4}$ Russians to 1 German. As the Germans had provisioned for 14:1 there was thus an overlap to decide the issue in the Russian favour.

A close parallel existed at Waterloo. Two entirely different methods of waging a battle were employed. Wellington (that is, all the allied forces except the Prussians) had his forces set out *in a line* facing the enemy (details to follow) whereas Napoleon's forces advanced *in column(s)*: so that, if an aerial view had been possible, the pattern would have seemed like a letter T, with Wellington's men crossing the upright formed by Napoleon's forces. Napoleon had superior numbers in this clash – but never, through his own misjudgment and mistakes, sufficiently superior numbers at the right place and the right time. As will be shown, at least twice he could have taken and sustained the initiative. As in the German v. Russia clash of 1941–42 the Germans simply did not have enough rifles, guns, aeroplanes, bombs, tanks, etc. to take on odds of $17\frac{1}{4}:1$; so, at Waterloo, there were never quite enough Frenchmen to overwhelm the English infantry and artillery.

Napoleon's basic blind spot in this affray was probably due to his inordinate conceit in his own military genius. He could admit – he could not avoid admitting – that Wellington and his army had certainly had some successes in the War of the Spanish Ulcer i.e. the Peninsular campaigns, but he could point out that (a) he had not been in Spain and (b) because of the terrain as well as other factors, the French there had not used 'heavy' cavalry. He seemed to be blind to the warnings given by his own advisers who, at peril of his displeasure, pointed out that Wellington had, at one time or another, defeated French forces led by Marshals Junot, Victor, Massena, Ney, Marmont, Jourdan and Soult.

Nevertheless, there was a point about the heavy cavalry. Light cavalry was used for reconnaissance, for pin-prick raids, for mopping-up after an infantry and/or artillery battle, and for equestrian heroics with dashing officers on comparatively lightweight sprint horses in the Prince Rupert tradition.

The 'heavy' cavalry meant great chargers mounted by heavily-armed riders who were intended to operate in a massed 'charge' at a canter, with lances and broad sabres thrusting and cutting. In practice, disciplined infantry had little to fear from such tactics if they formed squares and stood their ground. For the pending engagement with the British Napoleon carefully nursed his squadrons of heavy cavalry, as being – at least in theory – a 'trump card'.

Nor was Napoleon any the less confident as regards his infantry. He had ample evidence, seen with his own eyes, that the cold steel of a French bayonet charge was almost irresistible. The fact was that quite often his infantry had no need to *fire* their muskets, but went into action with fixed bayonets and, when opportunity offered, the muskets were used as great clubs. The mere sight of a fixed bayonet charge was enough to make most enemy soldiers break their ranks and run ... for the light cavalry to pursue and cut down.

Hence it must have been with wonder at his good luck that he observed the lines of defence drawn up by Wellington on the ridge just south of the village of Mont St. Jean because a narrow, restricted, front offered by the enemy was exactly what the French liked for their *modus operandi*.

In complement and contradistinction, Wellington must have felt great satisfaction at seeing the pre-battle formations of Napoleon because it was to have an enemy advancing in column formation that best suited British tactics.

Whether the point was appreciated or not at the time, the fact is that the French were following, with modern refinements, the pattern of the Macedonian phalanx type of warfare of around 550 B.C. whereas Wellington adopted the improved formula used by the Romans of the 1st Century B.C.

The Duke arranged his army in two lines, in parallel

along the ridge at Mont St. Jean, and had the reserves immediately behind. The lines were not straight: in plan view they wavered, following the line of the ridge, and each bend in the line actually assisted the infantry and gunners since it gave them position advantage for cross-fire.

Thus in theory all the advancing French column had to do was to penetrate the extended British lines at some point.

Consider the French method of attack, which was to employ the following general sequence:

Right out in front, in face of the enemy and (according to terrain and cover) perhaps as close as only 50 yards there was a screen of *tirailleurs* i.e. sharpshooters in loose and random array, firing at targets of opportunity. Necessarily they fired individually, often displayed great personal bravery in getting close to the enemy, and were expert at picking off such prizes as an officer commanding a gun battery.

The *tirailleurs*, often as thick as mayfly over a trout stream in summer, had three main functions:

1. To inflict casualties and thereby create disorder. As cited above, a battery commander was an ideal target.
2. To rattle off diversionary fire and to distract enemy attention from the real point of the attack which was about to be launched.
3. To cause penetrations of the enemy's line, or at least create weaknesses at pre-arranged points which would then be attacked by the follow-up infantry with a bayonet charge or the cavalry with a sabre or lances charge.

Behind, and in direct support of, the *tirailleurs* was the light artillery. Working together, the function of the artillery with the 'mosquito screen' was to create a weak-spot at a required position so that the infantry could go through on a fixed-bayonet charge and polish off the opposition.

The light artillery used what we now call antipersonnel attack, especially canister or case shot, which was musket balls packed into canisters which, on being fired, fragmented. Fire from light artillery could be quite devastating on a massed line of infantry, but the range was normally about 200 yards and hence inside the range of men with muskets.

Many wargamers will have seen the Royal Tournament display held in London each year, when teams compete in dismantling a field gun, taking it over an obstacle, then re-assembling it. That sort of operation was frequently seen in real battle: the light artillery teams could very rapidly set up a battery or remove it from capture by the enemy. This is a point that is of consequence in the progress of fighting at Waterloo.

The infantry advanced in column (column astern of the leader) under the protection of the *tirailleurs* and light infantry.

Les dragons (in English: the Dragoons) were originally mounted infantry i.e. they rode into battle but dismounted to fight, with sabres, alongside the infantry, but by the time of Waterloo they rated as medium cavalry and were used exclusively as such.

The heavy cavalry (mentioned above) were the *cuirassiers*. These cavalry soldiers wore a metal breastplate and back-plate positioned over a thick leather (*cuir*) jerkin, and a metal helmet. The *cuirassiers* moved *en masse*: they were drawn up and stationary, awaiting the signal to move forward. When they moved it was at first at a walk (so that the column could remain compact and not straggling), then at a trot, then a canter. It was the sheer weight of this type of charge that was supposed to carry everything before it, but in fact seldom did so.

There was one other factor that Wellington had taken note of in French tactics where Napoleon was in command. Up to about 1809, in, for example, the battles of Austerlitz (1805), Jena (1806) and to a lesser degree at Wagram (1809), Napoleon had used rapid manoeuvres to switch the point of an attack to another centre. But he had changed this formula to movements on a foreshortened and restricted front to enable concentration of artillery fire, and hence concentration for infantry or cavalry follow-up charges. At the same time, the notion of exploiting a sudden weakness was provided for by having the Imperial Guard held in a rear position to the first, frontal, attack so that it was ready for instant action at an order from the command post, moving thus without any delay to fight at a critical point with awful effect.

To recapitulate, long before the actual battle Wellington expected that:

1. The whole of his front line would be engaged by *tirailleurs* supported by light artillery and there would be fire 'over their heads' by the medium guns.
2. The infantry, in column(s), would attack weak points and would be supported by covering fire from the medium guns up to a maximum range of 1,000 yards.
3. The cavalry would exploit any weakness or wavering with direct charges.
4. The élite Imperial Guard would be held back as long as possible, and then, fresh to action, pour into the defence in massed formation.

Wellington's counter to the musketry of the *tirailleurs* was an opposing (and foremost) line of skirmishers, many armed with rifles and at least as numerous as the French. The very presence of these skirmishers automatically diminished the effectiveness of the *tirailleurs* who, necessarily, were so much the further geographically from their targets.

Furthermore, those skirmishers who were armed with the Baker flint-lock muzzle-load rifle had a maximum range of 450 yards, and an effective range of some 200 yards, so that the effect of the swarms of tirailleurs was much discounted by this weapon superiority in the key places where it existed.

Behind this front screen, the British and Allied infantry was intact in two extended lines. Fire was made in volleys, on command. Clearly, from their prepared firing position they had a distinct advantage over the

French troops on the move towards them. The British standard rate of fire was 16 seconds per volley. Firing was normally by half-companies in turn. Consequently, the leaders of any oncoming enemy column faced a withering concentration of fire and were shot down, as were their comrades who stepped forward to fill the breach. Inevitably, in time the advancing column was halted. As soon as that happened, the flanks of the defending line closed in on the enemy column which then had to suffer an overwhelming cross-fire.

With that as the basic pattern of the British and Allied tactics against infantry, now for the general method used against cavalry attack.

The lesson learned from earlier battles won by Napoleon was that the most dangerous attack would come from the French cuirassiers. The usual pattern of defence against cavalry attack was to form the infantry into 'squares' (each side 20 yards long). The front rank of each side of the square knelt to make a formidable line of bayonets fixed to the muskets, and from the row(s) behind this daunting hedge of steel came volley fire. And against this double-defence the enemy cavalry rarely pressed home direct charge on to the square, but, instead, horse and rider swerved aside to avoid being transfixed on the bayonets.

At Waterloo, with great expertise Wellington caused his artillery to be placed so that it could fire against both infantry and cavalry. The carefully worked out procedure was that when the enemy began to advance – and went through the motions preparatory to a charge – at that moment an expected order was given and the elongated and extended British front line would swiftly dissolve, to re-shape itself into a series of squares. On came the enemy cavalry, facing gusts of volleys, and in the last few seconds realising that ahead was a suddenly-created stockade of bayonets set up by muskets with butts on the ground. Hence, over and over again the charge of cavalry would sweep to either side of a square, perhaps vainly imagining that the British line had been

SUPPLY
RESERVES
C A V
C A V
W
C A V
SECOND LINE
Square
To form Square
Square
LINE
LINE
LINE
1 2 3 4 5 6 7 8 9
SHARP SHOOTERS
TIRAILLEURS
25 files wide
25 files wide
CAV
CAV
CAV
CAV
CAV
CAV
CAV
CAV
Old Guard 1
Old Guard 2
Young Guard
Middle Guard
N
IMPERIAL GUARD

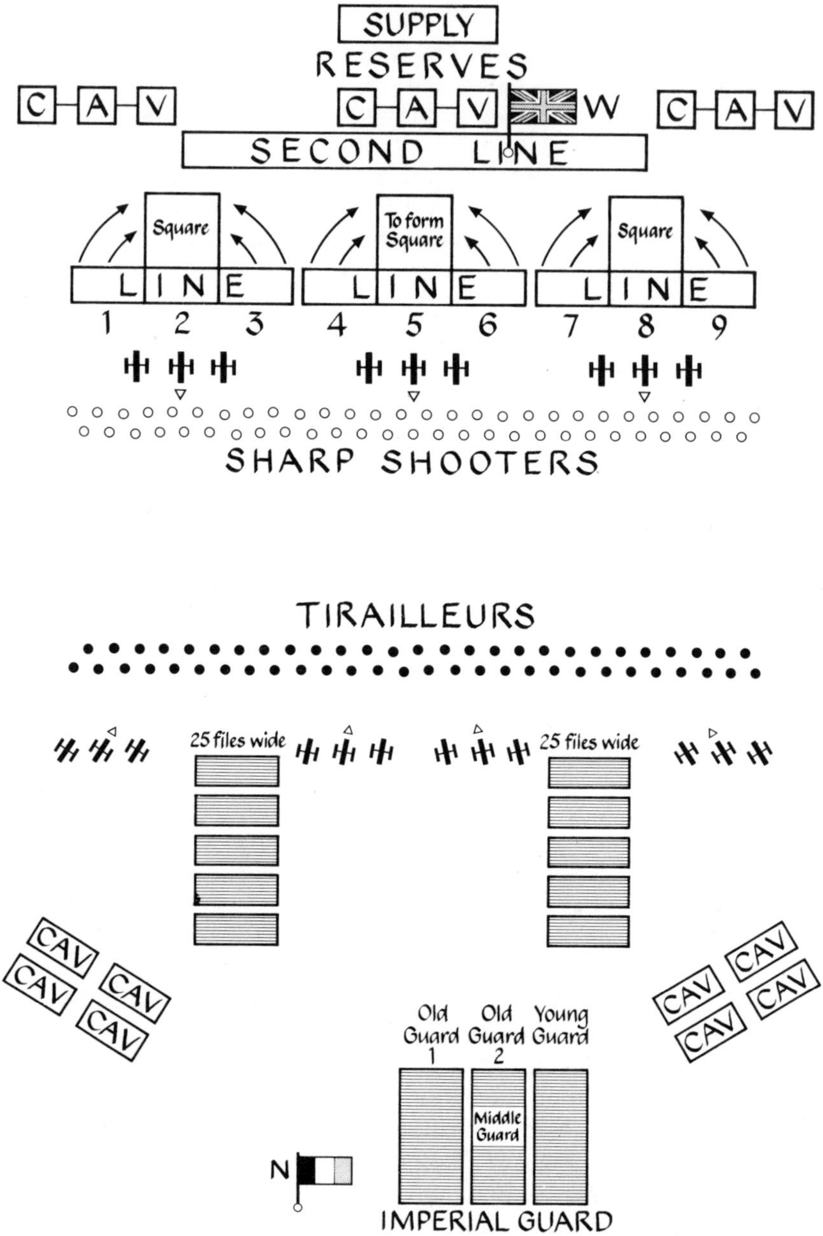

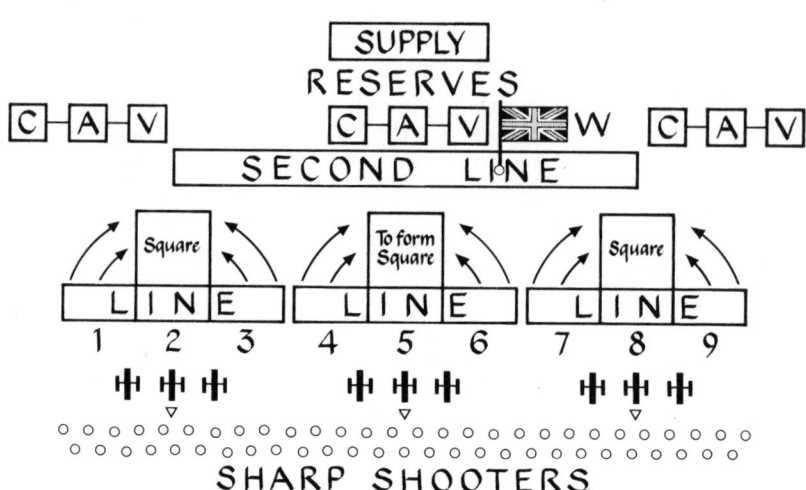

Fig. 3. Diagrammatic view of tactics employed at Waterloo

WELLINGTON *chose the ideal position, based on the features of the terrain. The front line was on the crest of the ridge, overlooking the shallow valley to the south. Maximum width of the front line was 1,600 yards.*

Each line could be dissolved on order to form squares: each square had a side of 20 yards. Cavalry advance round the lines or between the squares.

If the French charge the guns, the gunners drop back to the cover of the infantry behind them, and then resume their gun positions after the charge has (a) halted and then (b) been broken by the second line and the cavalry.

The sharpshooters are far enough forward to protect the gunners, to ensure enemy skirmishers and sharpshooters are kept out of range of the infantry line, and to pick off the leaders of advancing columns of the enemy.

NAPOLEON *needs the flat land of the valley to form up the squadrons of cavalry and huge columns of infantry.*

The French sharpshooters or Tirailleurs *swarm forward with the intention of picking off subordinate commanders with the allied guns or in the front line, and then to create weak points in that line.*

The Tirailleurs *have support from light mobile artillery which also aims to create weaknesses in the opposing line. When such a weakness is ready to be exploited, the infantry charge with bayonets fixed.*

The Imperial Guard is held back, not so much as a reserve as to be instantly ready to exploit any allied weakness. It marches in columns 25 men abreast.

broken. On the contrary, as the enemy cavalry swept by, so the sides of the squares fired at the horses and riders at point-blank range; and when the cavalry turned round to ride back to their own lines so once again came volley after volley from the squares . . . which then rapidly moved back into the original line.

None of this seems to have been appreciated by the French army, or by its commander; it is possible that, with a total disregard for loss of life, Napoleon realised there would be terrible losses against the British lines and squares but believed that he had sufficient numerical superiority to accept thousands of dead as, by sheer numbers, the French overwhelmed the defenders.

The plan so far outlined really covers but half the picture of a tactical defensive plan superbly thought-out long in advance.

It was so well thought out, indeed, that it might be said that if the battle had not been fought at the valley by Mont St. Jean then Wellington would have manoeuvred until he found another and exactly similar position elsewhere.

The *finesse* of the British position invokes unqualified admiration for Wellington's military genius because, being in the Brussels area in the summer of 1814, he came down the road to Charleroi and in a throw-away remark to his A.D.C. said then that if he had to fight the French he would try to do so from the ridge just south of the Forest of Soignes (i.e. where the battle actually was fought so many months later).

What he foresaw as to site was matched by his prescience of the pattern of action. His line was the crest of the hill; in fact, from any approach uphill from the valley it was just below a direct line of firing. Ahead of the infantry line were the field guns in batteries.

When the enemy infantry came on to attack, the vanguard skirmishers fell back to the shelter of the guns which blazed away at infantry unable to make effective reply.

When cavalry was brought in to deal with these

gunners, the tactics were as follows: the guns would be kept firing until the last minute, and then when the cavalry moved into a trot preparatory to the full charge the gunners would nip smartly back to the infantry squares magically forming up just behind them. The French cavalry would be allowed to overrun the forward guns from which the securing pin of a wheel had been extracted (or even a wheel completely removed) so that the enemy could not tow them away on the instant without again coming under close infantry fire, nor had they time and opportunity to spike a gun. When the cavalry charge had spent its impetus, and had ridden back to its start-point under cover of its infantry, then the English gunners nipped forward, replaced the the securing pins or wheels, and almost at once were again blasting away at the enemy. It was said, probably in exaggeration, that Wellington never lost a gun; certainly none were taken by the French from the fighting at the ridge of Mont St. Jean.

That, then, is the background pattern to the prolonged action, to the frequent French charges which as frequently fizzled out. The action developed into one of attrition – who would break first?

5
Sinews of War

It is perhaps somewhat glib and evasive of realities to speak merely of an army or a corps, citing just a number of men in each case. What has to be borne in mind is the enormous amount of equipment that went with an army.

Thus, the reader may have wondered a little when, on p. 17 it was stated that the Imperial Guard left Paris on 8th June and had moved only 125 miles (205 km.) N.E. by 13th June. This is a point-to-point overall transit speed of a mere 1 mile per hour, from noon to noon on the stated days, and it can be presumed that the slow progress was due to the enormous amount of equipment concerned.

It is difficult, probably impossible now, to give any true and fair indication of the amount of supplies needed for a Napoleonic army. However some notion of what Francis Bacon in an essay refers to as 'the sinews of war', can be gained from facts collected by Antony Brett-James in his informative work *Europe Against Napoleon* (Macmillan, 1970). The reference is to supplies from Britain to her continental allies, especially Russia and

Prussia, just before the battle of Leipzig (1813), from which period dates the decline and fall of Napoleon. The tally list is:

218 pieces of ordnance, complete with gun carriages and necessary field stores; plus rounds of ammunition, with suitable quantity of powder, wagons, etc.
124,119 stand of arms, with 18,231,000 rounds of ball cartridges, plus 23,000 barrels of powder, flints, etc.
34,443 swords, sabres, spears.
624 drums, trumpets, bugles, cavalry standards.
150,000 suits of clothing complete, plus greatcoats, cloaks, pelisses and overalls.
175,796 boots* and shoes, with leather for repairs.
114,000 blankets.
58,000 linen shirts and underpants.
87,190 pairs of gaiters.
69,624 pairs of stockings.
90,000 sets of accoutrements.
63,457 knapsacks complete.
14,820 saddles complete, with blankets.
100,000 caps and feathers.
22,000 forage caps.
14,000 stocks and clasps.
140,000 shoe-brushes, combs, and black-balls.
3,000 gloves and braces.
20,000 greatcoat straps, brushes, pickers, sponges, etc.
5,000 flannel shirts, gowns, caps and trowsers (sic).
14,000 sheets, paillasses, coverlids, etc.
5,000 haversacks and canteens complete.
702,000 lb. of biscuit and flour.
691,360 lb. of beef and pork.
28,625 gallons of brandy and rum.

In addition, there was a wide variety of marquees, tents, forage carts and camp equipment; surgical instru-

---

*The Wellington boot worn by European cavalrymen was (and is) known as the Blücher in Germany. During the Napoleonic Wars most boots worn by European armies (including the French) were made in Britain.

ments in cases, medicines, and all manner of general hospital stores, bandages, stretchers, splints, crutches, etc.

This formidable list of supplies is impressive not so much for the quantities involved but because of the tremendous variety of equipment indicated as necessary to conduct field operations.

Secret Weapons

The Royal Arsenal at Woolwich (Thames Estuary) was founded in 1720 in succession to an arsenal and dockyard dating back to Henry VIII. Part of the 18th Century establishment consisted of an experimental laboratory for development and testing of all manner of guns, mortars, bombs and other warlike stores and weapons.

In 1772 there was born to the wife of the Comptroller of the Royal Laboratory a son named William Congreve (who succeeded to the baronetcy in 1814). This son became an officer in the Royal Artillery in 1791, and was immediately detached to serve in the laboratory of which in fact he became Comptroller from 1814–28.

This officer-plus-backroom boy was an inventor of no mean merit. Being impressed by the inefficiency of artillery, especially as regards effective range, he applied his inventive mind to a rocket-propelled missile to replace the artillery projectile.

The Congreve Rocket was thus developed experimentally at Woolwich about 1803. As ever, the way of an inventor is hard, but in 1806 he staged a demonstration of fire which was witnessed by the then Prime Minister, William Pitt, and several ministers of the Cabinet. And on 6th October that year, Congreve Rockets were used in action for the first time in an attack on Boulogne, the town being set on fire by them. In this action 200 rockets were fired from only 18 boats.

Three years were to pass before Congreve received orders to prepare and equip two rocket companies; and in the waiting period, probably due to his own need for further experimentation in the then unknown science of aerodynamics, he produced a variety of weapons as variants on the main idea. The Congreve Rockets ranged from 8-pdr. to 32-pdr., the recommended piece for infantry support being the 12-pdr. which was readily portable and, with a range of up to 2,000 yards, capable in theory of out-shooting any piece of artillery of the period. The operation was more than a century ahead of its times: it required a hand-wheeled small cart for the heavy rockets and a portable tripod for the smaller. Each rocketman had four rockets as a standard kit – with the 12-pdrs. At the beginning of an action he would have one in his hand and three in a special back-pack. Using the portable frame and aided by an assistant, a rate of fire of four Congreves per minute was achieved on tests at Woolwich.

Doubtless, in the fashion of modern times when, for example, the jet aero-engine was regarded pre-War as a cranky piece of engineering from a very odd Cranwell cadet, so Congreve suffered disdain from the army and tolerant contempt for his development. However, though he was tied to the Laboratory at Woolwich he had in effect a collaborator in the field in the shape of Captain Richard Bogue, Royal Artillery, in command of the army's only rocketmen.

Congreve's invention made a sensational appearance on the first occasion it was given a combat chance. This was on 18th October, 1813, in the great battle for Leipzig ('the battle of all the nations'). To the east of the city by some 3 miles (5 km.) was the village of Paunsdorf, strongly held by the French who had repulsed repeated attacks by Prussian troops of General Bülow's corps. Captain Bogue asked permission to have a go, and moved his Troop of only 200 Rocketmen into close range under the French guns and muskets. Fire was opened with devastating effect. Witnesses of the destruction and carnage caused by the Congreves later spoke of the hissing horrors that fried men alive, and of the diabolical and astonishing development in warfare as a solid square of infantry was paralysed solid, then burned as it collapsed and fled. In less dramatic terms, a mere 200 Rocketmen routed no fewer than 5 enemy battalions (some 2,500 men) and the strongly-defended outpost at Paunsdorf fell to the Prussians though a stray shot killed the gallant British Captain instantly.

Presumably the Department of War in London considered that Wellington, with a string of victories in Spain, should avail himself of the new weapon which only the British had so far. A demonstration of fire was laid on at St. Jean de Luz (just across the frontier from Spain, in the S.W. corner of France). There the display was extremely disappointing. The onlookers, including the Duke himself, were impressed by the devilish noise which would certainly stampede cavalry, but as an assault weapon the rockets proved to be erratic in both direction and range, and some merely ricocheted almost harmlessly along the ground. As a demonstration it was a flop – one can only assume that without their gallant but dead Captain Bogue the Rocketmen did not come up to scratch. At any rate, Wellington moved on, and though immediately ahead lay the assaults on Bayonne and Toulouse the Congreves were not employed in those actions. Nor, with the run-down of arms that followed Napoleon's first abdication (1814) was there any further development of or encouragement for Congreve's invention. When, suddenly, in the 100 Days there was a war once again the Congreve weapons were in very short supply. Some were fired at Waterloo, but far too few to be of any significance in the battle. On the whole they proved inaccurate and as dangerous to those firing them as to those at whom they were aimed.

So Waterloo was won without the help of a secret weapon – but what a fascinating 'might-have-been' can be built around Congreve and the brave Captain Bogue.

There are further puzzles likely now to be forever without positive explanation. For example, as early as 1800 an Englishman named Ezekiel Baker had developed a rifle which had passed tests at Woolwich

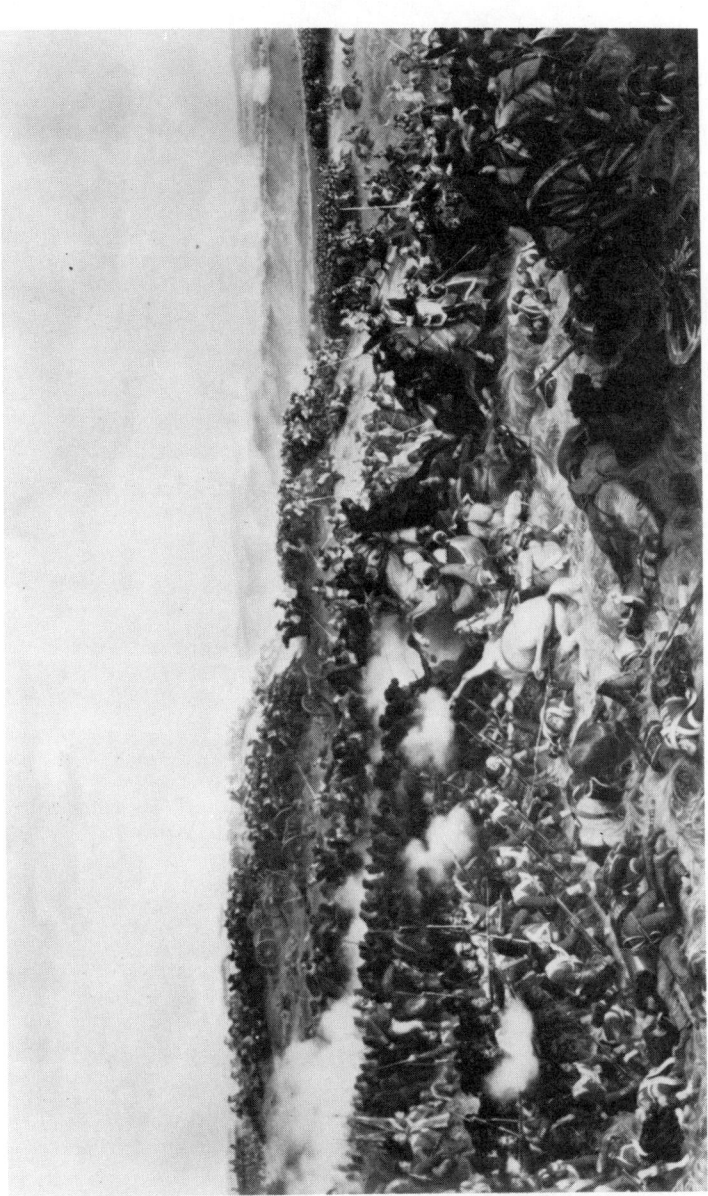

Plate 7 Felix Philippoteaux's famous panoramic painting of the charge of the French Heavy cavalry at Waterloo.

Plate 8 Marshal Ney, in command of the French left wing

Plate 9 Napoleon's Chief of Staff at Waterloo, the veteran Marshal Soult, Duke of Dalmatia

Plate 10 Lieut.-General Sir Thomas Picton, G.C.B.

Plate 11 View from Mont St. Jean at the commencement of the final allied charge on the demoralised French, at about 7 o'clock in the evening of the 18th June, 1815. From a print dated 1816

Plate 12 The famous meeting of Wellington and Blücher at La Belle Alliance *after the battle. After the painting by Maclise*

Plate 13 Feldmarschall Gebhard Leberecht von Blücher

Arsenal. It was 30 inches long in the barrel, and the rifling was quarter-turn seven groove. Its calibre (i.e. bore) was 0.625 in. It had a cheek rest, and a brass pistol-grip trigger guard. It weighed 9 lb. and had an effective range of 200 yards. With it was also a brass butt box to hold bullet patches and rammer tools.

In addition, there was the Baker bayonet. This was a flat sword type, with single-edged blade. It was 23 inches long, weighed 2 lb. and admittedly, in its original pattern, had a clumsy attachment.

The Baker rifle was used by the Rifle Corps long before Waterloo; and in service conditions it could be fired at one round per minute. It was, as a firearm, far superior to the musket, and yet as long as 15 years after its first official approval it was still not available in any quantity for Wellington's infantry.

The whole story of the development of the rifle is a mystery because from the start it was recognised as superior to the musket in accuracy and range. (It is a simple matter of dynamics to show that the spin imparted by rifling must give far greater stability in flight than that of a ball fired through a smooth bore musket.)

The rifle probably dates to a Danish development of 1611. In 1742 a learned treatise on the subject was presented to the Royal Society. Furthermore, in the American War of Independence (1775–81) rifles of the British Ferguson breech-loading type were proved over and again superior to a variety of muzzle-loaders. So why, for decades, was the rifle ignored in the main by the British army? What a difference it could have made at Waterloo.

The Imperial Guard

This élite force was the special creation of Napoleon in 1804 when he became Emperor.

It should not be confused with the National Guard, which was formed as a sort of citizens' army at Paris in 1789 in the early days of the Revolution.

The original Imperial Guard was a formal military

body attached to, and under the direct control of, the Emperor. When founded, it totalled 9,775 officers and men. Thereafter it steadily increased in size, until at one time its *paper* strength was 102,706 all ranks. However, at the time of Waterloo its strength was very much less than this – and not all the Guard were present at the battle.

At Waterloo on 18th June, the Imperial Guard was in three sections:

1. The Old Guard, of veterans, commanded by General Friant. This comprised:
    2 Regiments of Grenadiers
    2 Regiments of Chasseurs

Note that the word *chasseur* has changed in meaning in modern times. Today it is applied to fighter aircraft and to hunter submarines, for example, but in the first part of the 19th Century it meant Light Infantry – although the word *Chasseurs* was also used as an abbreviation for *Chasseurs à Cheval* which meant Light Cavalry.

2. The Middle Guard, commanded by General Count Morand. This had the same complement as the Old Guard, but had less experienced and mainly younger personnel.

3. The Young Guard, commanded by General Duhesme, made up of:
    2 Regiments of *voltigeurs* (specialist Light Infantry)
    2 Regiments of *tirailleurs* (sharpshooters).

That was the hard core of this formidable force. On the right (in battle formation) were the light cavalry and lancers with the infantry to their left; and on the left were grenadiers and dragoons with the infantry on their right.

An estimated grand total of the Guard at Waterloo is 20,000 total, but that could be much on the high side.

The remainder of the Imperial Guard was partly in Paris and partly in La Vendée, the politically active zone of Western France in the area between Nantes and La Rochelle on the Atlantic coast.

Of course, records were in a fine old tangle in the aftermath of Waterloo, and, as regards the Guard, are further bedevilled by the fact that one of the first acts of Louis XVIII on his second Restoration in 1815 was to disband the élite force which had been so much committed to the interests of Napoleon.

For that reason the references to the Imperial Guard in this narrative are based on generally accepted historical opinion – but bear in mind that the researcher often discovers, but must not be put off by, discrepancies in detail. Thus, the Young Guard is positively identified as being commanded by General Duhesme in (for example) the account by the historian Sir Edward Creasy but in the translation and interpretation of the account given by Blücher, the commanding officer is named as Lt.-General Barrois.

Furthermore, in place of Creasy's Old, Middle and Young Guards the German report lists Old Guard 1st and 2nd Divisions, and then the Young Guard. Likewise, there is occasional reference to General Friaud instead of Friant.

A note on rank

Although the rank or title of Marshal (or, in French, *Maréchal*) is frequently used, there is a degree of imprecision as to exactly what it meant beyond, probably, a general who had won a major victory on the battlefield.

Originally, marshals in both England and France were of ancient and royal privilege. In England the Marshal evolved into a feudal dignitary at court, whose duties were somewhere between a Master of Ceremonies and a Master of Horse. He became the premier knight of chivalry, like William Marshal, Earl of Pembroke, present at Runnymede in support of King John in 1215, and so commander of the royal army. The Earl Marshal of England (Duke of Norfolk) embodies this courtly supremacy today.

Application of the term to the purely military came as late as 1736 when George II promoted the Duke of

Argyll and the Earl of Orkney to the rank of Field Marshal. Wellington was made a Field Marshal in 1813, and his was the only such title in the British Army during his war years. (Later, members of the royal family acquired the title in order to out-rank any commoner in the military service.)

In France, marshals were originally esquires to the king, and acted (a) as observers for the king, being in the vanguard of an action, or (b) as types of quarter-master or billeting officer, going ahead to chose the place for encampment or lodging. The status of a *maréchal* in the 15th Century was that of a Court official: there were only two, and they received 500 livres per annum in war but nothing in peace. That was changed in the reign of Francois I (1515–47), and the first definite appointment of military *maréchal*s came in the reign of Louis XIV (1638–1715). Napoleon seems to have awarded the title to any of his generals who were victorious in a battle – rather like a sort of Honours Cap in Rugby Football; and often the honour was accompanied by a dukedom. The fact is that the term does not appear as a military rank in the lists of those who led the French at Waterloo.

In the records, Napoleon stands as Commander-in-Chief, and all of his subordinate commanders are Generals of Division or Generals of Brigade.

To make the position as clear as possible, here is the scale of rank equivalents:

English	*French*
Field Marshal	Napoleon (Commander-in-Chief)
General	General of Division
Lieutenant-General	General of Brigade
Major-General	General of Brigade
Colonel	Colonel

Napoleon's Marshals

Napoleon revived the title of marshal during the war period 1804–14. As confusion could arise due to reference to a marshal under his civil title as well as, or

in lieu, of his military title, here is a selection of the better known who were still active in 1815:
(In alphabetical order)

Brune, Guillaume. He was murdered at Avignon 2nd August, 1815, in *La Terreur Blanche*, i.e. revenge by the restored aristos.

Davout, Louis Nicolas. Prince of Eckmuhl, Duke of Auerstadt. He was born in 1770 at Annoux, and died 1st June, 1823.

Grouchy, Emmanuel. Listed as *Emmanuel, Marquis de Grouchy*. Born in the Château de Villete (Ile de France) in 1766, and died 29th May, 1847.

Jourdan, Jean Baptiste. Born at Limoges in 1762. Became a peer of France under Louis XVIII, and Governor of Les Invalides under Louis-Philippe. He died 23rd November, 1833.

Kellermann, François Christophe. Duke of Valmy. Born at Strasbourg in 1735; died 12th September, 1820. Not to be confused with his son, François Etienne Kellermann (1770–1835) who fought at Waterloo.

Lefebvre, Francois Joseph. Duke of Dantzig (now called Gdansk). Born at Rouffach in 1755, died 14th September, 1820. His wife, who had been a laundry-woman, was popularised by the dramatist Victorien Sardou as Madame Sans-Gêne.

Macdonald, Alexandre. Duke of Taranto. He was born at Sedan in 1765, and was the officer who negotiated with the allies for the abdication of Napoleon. He died 24th September, 1840.

Marmont, Auguste Viesse de. Duke of Ragusa. Born 1774. One of the marshals who negotiated for Napoleon's abdication. He died 2nd March, 1852.

Massena, André. Prince of Essling, and Duke of Rivoli. Born at Nice in 1758. After Wagram in 1809 Napoleon proclaimed him *L'Enfant Chéri de la Victoire*. He died 4th April, 1817.

Moncey, Bon Adrien Jeannot de. Duke of Conegliano. Born 1754, he was a Peninsular War general and defended Paris in 1814. He died 20th April, 1842.

Murat, Joachim. Grand Duke of Berg and of Cleves, and from 1808 King of Naples. Being obliged to quit this throne when Napoleon (his brother-in-law) fell, he attempted to reconquer it but was captured at Pizza and shot by an execution squad on 13th October, 1815.

Ney, Michel. Prince of Moscow, Duke of Elchingen. Born at Sarrelouis in 1769, he was known for his battle feats as 'the bravest of the brave'. After Napoleon's first abdication (1814) Louis XVIII made him a Peer of France. When Napoleon escaped from Elba, Ney rejoined him and fought at Waterloo. After the second abdication, and second Restoration, Ney was arraigned for treason, condemned to death by the Court of Peers, and executed by firing squad on the 7th December, 1815.

Soult, Nicolas. Duke of Dalmatia. Born in 1769 at Saint-Amans-la-Bastide, he turned to politics in a career somewhat parallel to that of Wellington post 1815. He died 26th November, 1851.

Victor, Claude Perrin. Duke of Belluno. Born at Lamarche in Lorraine in 1764, his original surname was Perrin. He died 1st March, 1841.

6
Among Those Present...

As everyone with experience knows, even from the most seemingly trustworthy of people evidence must be suspect. It is extraordinary and beyond rational explanation that two people can view precisely the same incident and later give different, sometimes conflicting accounts of what they assert they saw.

That warning is as necessary with regard to Waterloo as with any other major event of history. Apart from the immediate despatches, of which one example is quoted on p. 143, the historians did not really get their teeth into the Waterloo campaign until the 1840's. There was then published in 1844 a 2-volume work entitled *The History of the Waterloo Campaign*, cited in the *Dictionary of National Biography* as *History of the War in France and Belgium in 1815*, and written by Captain William Siborne. This officer served with the 9th Foot in the Army of Occupation 1815–17; and he achieved considerable acclaim for his construction of a model of the field of battle, erected in the United Service Institution (given royal charter status in 1860) during the years

1830–38. Captain Siborne was employed as a subordinate military secretary 1826–43, and clearly the duties were not sufficiently arduous to debar him from his pet subject; so that in 1844, released from the army and made Secretary of the military hospital at Chelsea, he was able to publish his work on Waterloo.

How much reliance was placed on Siborne's works by Sir Edward Creasy cannot be known, but as a professional historian (with the chair in history at London University) it is unlikely that the earlier source was ignored by Creasy when preparing his account published in 1851. Neither of these narrators seems to have been aware of the discrepancies in the figures – variously quoted as to the size of the forces.

The truth is that all precise figures on the scale of the action at Waterloo should be suspect. It is almost impossible not to duplicate counting in places and, as anyone with Service experience will confirm, an officer or man may truly be on the books as being at place A whilst that same person is temporarily and lawfully somewhere else (on a course, on leave, in the sick bay at base, and so on). What is certain is that only part of the gross forces available actually fought at Waterloo.

An example of a possible cause for discrepancy concerns the force of the Prince of Orange which, on the final day of 18th June, was positioned astride the Nivelles road *to which Napoleon might well have switched* his left flank had the Prussian thrust on the French right been more positive. At a certain stage this force was not in the fighting, but it very easily could have been.

Another possible cause of confusion is that in 1815 the British monarch was George III (mentally sick, in degenerative old age) with the Regent as the *ad hoc* head of the State and also the House of Hanover. One has to remember therefore that the Germans of Prussia (then with their own king) were entirely separate from the German troops from George III's Hanoverian territory who were generally accepted as part of the 'British' forces.

Those qualifications must be borne in mind when reading figures of forces at Waterloo. So:

The grand total of 'British' forces in the Brussels/Waterloo area in the first week of June, 1815, was 43,939. This figure is sometimes cited for 'British and Hanoverians in Flanders'.

Its total included:

Cavalry	8,883
Artillery	5,434
Infantry	29,622
	43,939

Breaking down the total of 29,622 for Infantry we have figures for the Hanoverians:

Plat's Brigade, King's German Legion	1,790
Halket's Brigade, Hanoverians	2,235
Col. Ompteda's King's German Legion	1,704
Count Kielmansegge's Hanoverians	2,472
Col. Vincke ditto	2,260
Col. Best ditto	2,345
	12,806

To this total of men we would now regard as 'foreigners', should be added figures for the English forces at the Battles of Quatre Bras and Waterloo:

Cavalry	6,170
Infantry	16,816
	22,986

This figure is the nearest to the oft-quoted 'fewer than 24,000 English fought against Napoleon at Waterloo'. Vaguely correct, but of course this total includes the Scots, the Welsh and the Irish Regiments who fought alongside the English. However, for the 'British' total, (which means excluding the Belgians, Dutch, etc.) we must add in the Hanoverian cavalry (2,713) which gives the Hanoverians a total of 15,519 men . . . and a grand

'British' total of 38,505. Compare this with Creasy's statement of overall allied strength at Waterloo:

Infantry	49,608	
Cavalry	12,402	
Artillery	5,645	(with 156 guns)
	67,655	

of which (see above) 'scarcely 24,000 were English'.

It is reasonable to suppose that even Wellington did not know, at the time, the numerical strength of the Prussians under Blücher, who had undertaken to supply the Duke with 25,000 men.

However, with hindsight and the usual caution as to figure accuracy, the records show Feldmarschall Gebhard Leberecht von Blücher, Prince von Wahlstadt as overall commander of all troops of the Prussian forces *in this area* (the point is a valid one to make: had Blücher's entire force been wiped out, there were other army corps still left to fight Napoleon and avenge Jena and Auerstadt).

Blücher's right hand man in every sense was Lt.-General Count von Gneisenau, who was Chief of Staff. Gneisenau had commanded Prussian soldiers on the English side in the American War of Independence (1782). He distrusted British generals and had a low estimate of Wellington. He was accused of causing the delay in linking up with the British after Ligny, but achieved a miracle of reorganisation after that defeat.

Beneath Gneisenau was Major-General Karl von Grölmann who was Quartermaster General.

As personal representative of Blücher and Liaison Officer with the Duke of Wellington there was, as already mentioned, Major-General Baron von Müffling.

The grand totals of the several corps under Blücher were:

Infantry	136 battalions	105,871
Cavalry	135 squadrons	11,948

Artillery	38 batteries	4,861
Pioneers		492
		123,172

Blücher had in his total force of artillery 304 guns, but in the actual fighting – in the critical actions as they directly affected issues at and just before Waterloo – he confronted Napoleon's forces with 83,417 men and 224 guns. Note that that figure specifically does *not* include the 25,000 men of General Bülow's 4th Corps which was far away *when the series of battles started*, but which came into action later.

However, when assessing the forces of Napoleon and Wellington in direct confrontation south of Mont St. Jean, the wargamer should remember the following fact (which will be described in detail in due course): when Napoleon gave orders for the defeated Prussians to be pursued by his right wing he effectively *detached* some 32,000 troops and 96 guns in the vain chase made by Marshal Grouchy.

Now for the total forces available to Napoleon. In the overall area, and including the zones with fortresses and garrisons from which he made his initial concentrations, Napoleon had available some 150,000 men.

According to Captain Siborne, whom Creasy and others cite, Napoleon's army at Waterloo totalled

Infantry	48,950
Cavalry	15,765
Artillery	7,232
	71,947

He is also credited with 246 guns.

Wellington (see above) is credited with 156 guns.

Now, if you subtract the 96 guns that Napoleon detached from his total of 246 guns, he was left with 150 guns, or almost exactly the English total.

Despite those figures, in an Order of Battle made by Wellington there is the following footnote:

'Artillery, commanded by Colonel Sir George Wood, comprised 30 brigades, each of six guns.'

Simple arithmetic gives thus a total of 180 guns for Wellington.

The point for the wargamer to note is that all the guns of all the combatants were mostly 6-pdr or 12-pdr, and no authority states what the totals were for each. One set of figures does, however, give a slight guide in this matter: one of the Prussian cavalry Divisions had two batteries of 12-pdr guns plus six batteries of 6-pdr guns used to support dragoons and hussars.

Of course, whatever the figures were or were not when the action started, they rapidly changed under the impact of tremendous casualties. Here, again, any attempt at accuracy is doomed to failure. Sir Edward Creasy states categorically and bluntly: 'No returns ever were made of the amount of the French loss in the battle of Waterloo; but it must have been immense, and may be partially judged by the amount of killed and wounded in the armies of the conquerors. . . .'

That authoritative and encyclopaedic compiler of information, Joseph Haydn, whose memorable work first appeared in 1841, states as follows:

'Of the British (23,991), 93 officers and 1,916 men were killed or missing; and 363 officers and 4,560 men wounded – total 6,932; and the total loss of the allied army amounted to 4,206 killed, 14,539 wounded and 4,231 missing, making 22,976 *hors de combat*.'

There is, however, another set of figures, equally fascinating and illuminating in their own way since, although they disagree with the professional historian, Creasy, and also those of Haydn, they are not so different in general as to make nonsense of the others. Yet they are a biting commentary on all such statistics. Captain W. Siborne (writing long years after the event although he may well have gathered the information during his spell in the army of occupation of France, 1815–17) states that *at Waterloo* the casualties were:

```
Killed    1,319 horses and 1,245 soldiers below the rank of Sergeant
Wounded    719      ,,        4,261     ,,        ,,          ,,
Missing    708      ,,          558     ,,        ,,          ,,
```

Imagination baulks and boggles at the notion of 500 + men and 700 + horses vanishing ... were they really blown to unidentifiable pieces without being noticed and recorded by someone, or did they just disappear from the battle scene, bolting before the cannons and without anybody noticing they were tearing off the battlefield?

For the wargamer there are yet more figures which open up exciting possibilities.

First, to quote Creasy in his general description of the opposing forces:

'In the Emperor's own words, speaking of this campaign, "a French soldier would not be equal to more than one English soldier, but he would not be afraid to meet two Dutchmen, Prussians, or soldiers of the Confederation." There were about 6,000 men, of the old German Legion, with the Duke; these were veteran troops and of excellent quality. Of the rest of the army the Hanoverians and Brunswickers proved themselves deserving of confidence and praise. But the Nassauers, Dutch and Belgians were almost worthless; and not a few of them were justly suspected of a strong wish to fight, if they fought at all, under the French eagles rather than against them.'

One wonders however if the historian of 1851 was fully aware of the situation existing in 1815. The basic fact is that the Belgians wanted independence above everything, and not, as seemed likely, compulsory amalgamation with the Dutch in a swollen United Netherlands. Likewise, many of the Dutch did not want political entanglement with the running sore of Flanders, a scene of almost constant warfare for at least 1,000 years before Waterloo.

Bearing that in mind, Captain Siborne has this to say of the twelve Dutch-Belgian battalions:

'Half were with difficulty prevented from abandoning the field although at that moment they were not in contact with, nor did they even see, the enemy . . .

'And half only joined the front line (left of Maitland's Brigade) at the time of the general advance.'

Siborne cites the total Dutch-Belgian forces in comparison with the English (and, again, the totals do not quite line up with figures given earlier) as:

Infantry: 13,402 (cf. British 15,181)
Cavalry: 3,205 (,, ,, 5,843)
Guns: 32 (,, ,, 78)

With heavy sarcasm Siborne comments that it is needless to speculate how the battle would have been changed if these considerable forces had pulled their full weight.

However, their very existence does present the wargamer with a splendid chance to exercise skill and judgment. Were these troops geared to stick together as the English did would they not have been the vital weakness for which Napoleon was ever ready to probe . . . and then pour in the Imperial Guard? This is just another imponderable of the great battle of Waterloo.

7
Order of Battle
◆◆◆

In order to give reasonable position fixes of the troops in action at Waterloo it is desirable to have a datum-line. The most convenient is the Brussels–Charleroi highway that traversed from north to south the battlefield that was itself in general on an east–west orientation.

For convenience the blanket term used for the allied forces, unless specifically identified, is 'English'.

Unhappily the military term 'Division' has, in different armies and at different times, meant many different things; and, indeed, in modern times an armoured division differs in complement materially from an infantry division, whilst the modern English, American, Russian, and other foreign armies each have their particular scale of numbers for their respective versions of the 'division'.

At Waterloo, four English (i.e. English commanded) divisions were involved in the fighting. There was another division in Belgium, commanded by Lt.-General Sir Charles Colville (1770–1843), but that was elsewhere on 18th June, 1815.

Before tabulating the four divisions, it has to be understood that each had its quota of artillery support, as well as Engineers. The Corps of Engineers was the youngest section of the army; it was formed as late as 25th April, 1787, as a military component of the army under a Colonel-in-Chief, and it ranked level with the Artillery. Originally incorporated with the Artillery, it shared its motto *Ubique* (Everywhere).

The Artillery was dispersed throughout the entire English army, and was under the corps command of Colonel Sir George Adam Wood (1767–1831) who was later promoted Major-General.

The Engineers were under the corps command of Colonel James Carmichael Smyth who had entered the Artillery from Woolwich in 1794 and transferred to the Engineers in 1795. He was created 1st baronet in 1821 for conspicuous military services, and preferred to be known not for his army career but as Governor of British Guiana. He lived 1779–1838.

The pattern I have followed in detailing the various divisions is to give the overall commander; then the corps commander; then the composition of the corps; then the regiments involved. Of the senior officers named, four were killed and seven were wounded, their names being marked (K) or (W) as appropriate.

1ST CORPS, commanded by General H.R.H. the Prince of Orange (W), had 2 divisions, identified as the 1st and 3rd.

1st Division
Commanded by Major-General (Sir) George Cooke (1768–1837), knighted after Waterloo. The division consisted of:

(1) The 1st British Brigade, consisting of the 1st and 3rd Regiments of Guards, commanded by Major-General (Sir) Peregrine Maitland (1777–1854), also knighted after Waterloo,

(2) 2nd British Brigade, 2nd and 3rd Guards, under

Major-General Sir John Byng (1772–1860), later Field Marshal the Earl of Stafford.

3rd Division
Commanded by Lt.-General Baron Sir Charles Alten (1764–1840) (W). This title needs explanation: Count von Alten served in the Hanoverian Army 1781–1803, and on its disbandment he transferred to the British Army which he served (1805–15) changing his title of Count to Baron. Long after Waterloo he became a Field Marshal in the re-organised Hanoverian Army. His command consisted of:

(1) The 5th British Brigade, Major-General Sir Colin Halkett (1774–1856) (W). Halkett began his career in the Dutch foot-guards 1792–95 in British pay, then served in the German Legion 1805–6, and led the German brigade in battles in the Peninsular War. At Waterloo he had the 30th, 33rd, 69th and 73rd Regiments. Note that the 33rd was Wellington's original career regiment.

(2) The 1st British Brigade of the King's German Legion, under command of Colonel the Baron Ompteda (K), and (3) the 1st Hanoverian Brigade under Colonel Kielmansegge, with the former having the 5th, 8th, 12th Regiments and Light Battalion, and the latter the Duke of York's Regiment with Hanoverian troops.

2ND CORPS, commanded by Lt.-General Baron Hill (1772–1842). Rowland Hill entered the Strasbourg military school as a subaltern, and as a Major-General had a brilliant series of successes in the Peninsular War, being created a Baron in 1814 and given a pension of £2,000 a year. In 1815 he was sent on a mission to the Prince of Orange, and later given command of an army corps in Belgium. He is cited as heading the charge ordered by Major-General Adam (his subordinate!) in the last decisive action on the battlefield at Waterloo. He became C. in C. the army in England, 1825–39, and was created 1st Viscount in 1842.

2nd Division
Commanded by Lt.-General Sir Henry Clinton (1771–1829), a Russian army expert who had command of a division in the Peninsular War. He commanded:
(1) The 3rd British Brigade under Major-General (Sir) Frederick Adam (1781–1853), knighted after Waterloo (W).
(2) Major-General Du Plat (K) with the 1st Brigade of the King's German Legion, and (3) the 3rd Hanoverian Brigade with part of the 4th Hanoverians, commanded by Colonel Halkett (W). Hugh Halkett, otherwise Baron Halkett, was a General in the Hanoverian army and a Colonel in the British. He had served in India with a Scottish Brigade, and organised levies and militia in Germany 1813–15. It was Halkett who, though wounded, captured the French General Pierre Cambronne who was commanding a last stand fight by a square of the Old Guard.
Clinton's 2nd Divison comprised the 52nd, 71st and 95th English regiments, and the 1st, 2nd, 3rd and 4th Hanoverians.

5th Division
Commanded by Lt.-General Sir Thomas Picton (1758–1815) (K). Picton was a famous soldier from the time he entered the 12th Foot in 1771. He was thanked seven times by the House of Commons for his services in the Peninsular War. He was wounded in the action at Quatre Bras, and then killed whilst leading a Brigade to the charge at Waterloo. He had under his command:
(1) The 8th British Brigade, commanded by Major-General (Sir) James Kempt (1764–1854), (W), who took over command of Picton's division when he was killed. Kempt was knighted after Waterloo, and rose to be Master-General of the Ordnance, 1834–38. With Kempt were the 28th, 32nd, 79th and 95th British Regiments.
(2) The 9th British Brigade, under Major-General Sir Denis Pack (1772–1823) in command of the 42nd,

44th and 92nd Regiments, and (3) the 5th Hanoverian Brigade under Colonel Vincke.

The Cavalry was under the overall command of a splendidly colourful character named Henry William Paget, 1st Marquess of Anglesey and 2nd Earl of Uxbridge of the Second creation. Generally referred to in connexion with Waterloo as Lord Uxbridge (1768–1854) (W), he commanded the cavalry with great distinction in Spain under Sir John Moore, and the cavalry and horse artillery at Waterloo where he lost a leg (see p. 167). He was created Marquis of Anglesey after Waterloo and promoted Field Marshal in 1846.

There were eight cavalry commands under Lord Uxbridge:
1. Major-General Lord Edward Somerset (1776–1842). His formal name was Lord Robert Edward Henry Somerset, a member of the Beaufort family. He had under command the 1st Brigade of 1st and 2nd Life Guards, the 1st Dragoon Guards, and the Horse Guards (The Blues).
2. Major-General Sir William Ponsonby (1772–1815) (K) with the 1st, 2nd and 6th Dragoons; he led the Brigade charge on the troops of Count d'Erlon, delivering a shattering attack which led to the main force collapse. Unfortunately this officer – described by Wellington as 'an ornament to his profession' – was killed by French lancers.
3. The 1st and 2nd Light Dragoons of the King's German Legion, and the 23rd Regiment of English Light Dragoons, commanded by Major-General Count Dornberg (W).
4. The 11th, 12th and 16th Light Dragoons, commanded by Major-General (Sir) John Ormsby Vandeleur (1763–1849), knighted after Waterloo. He began his career as an infantry officer in 1781; exchanged into the dragoons in 1792; commanded an infantry brigade in Spain in 1811, then an infantry division 1812–13, then

a cavalry brigade in 1813, and the 4th Cavalry Brigade at Waterloo. He was promoted General in 1838.

5. Major-General Sir Colquhoun Grant (1764–1835) had the 2nd, 7th and 15th Hussars. Should not be confused with Lt. Colonel Colquhoun Grant (1780–1829), a highly successful intelligence officer who warned Wellington of Napoleon's intentions before Waterloo.

6. The 6th Brigade, made up of the 1st, 10th and 18th Hussars, was under Major-General Sir (Richard) Hussey Vivian (1775–1842), created Baron Vivian in 1841.

7. The 3rd Hussars and 13th Light Dragoons were under command of Colonel Baron de Aerenschildt.

8. Colonel Estorff had cavalry of the Prince Regent Regiment, the Bremen Regiment, the Verdun Regiment, and the Cumberland Hussars.

Other distinguished officers later mentioned in despatches were:

Lt.-Colonel Sir Alexander Gordon (1786–1815) (K), who was A.D.C. to Wellington in the Peninsula and in Belgium. He was mortally wounded.

Major-General Sir Edward Barnes (1776–1838) (W), who served as Adjutant-General to the Forces at Waterloo.

In the account of the battle which follows, care should be taken to distinguish between Major-General Sir William Ponsonby who was killed (see above, under the cavalry), and Major-General Sir Frederick Cavendish Ponsonby (1783–1837) who at Waterloo was Colonel the Hon. Frederick Ponsonby, wounded, and knighted much later.

Lord Edward Somerset (see above, cavalry).

Lt.-Colonel Lord Fitzroy Somerset (1788–1855) who lost an arm when in close attendance on Wellington at Waterloo. This Somerset was the youngest son of the 5th Duke of Beaufort, and later became 1st Baron Raglan (blamed by some for the blunder of the Light Brigade charge at Balaclava in 1854).

General H.R.H. the Prince of Orange, severely wounded, who was with the Reserve on the left of Lt.-General Lord Hill's 2nd Corps and close to Wellington's command post, near Mont Saint Jean.

Prince Frederick of Orange who was on the right of Lord Hill, with 18,000 troops athwart the Mons–Brussels highway at Halle. This force was a vital barrier to a break-away by Napoleon on the French left, but it did not enter into the main action at Waterloo.

It is appropriate to point out here that on the French side there was a general named (in full) Jean Baptiste Drouet, Comte d'Erlon. This officer is often referred to as Erlon, or Count d'Erlon, or else Drouet. In the modern *Petit Larousse* he is entered as Drouet; in Creasy's famous history he is listed as D'Erlon; and in the modern *Encyclopedia Britannica* he appears as Drouet d'Erlon.

Some other names of interest are:

Brevet-Colonel John Gurwood (1790–1845) who is mainly known as the Editor of Wellington's Despatches on which he worked 1837–44 whilst being private secretary to the Duke. He was a subaltern in Spain when badly wounded in 1812; then exchanged into the cavalry; became A.D.C. to Lt.-General Sir Henry Clinton (later with 2nd Division) and was again wounded, in action at Waterloo.

His Serene Highness, Frederick William, Duke of Brunswick (1771–1815). He was the brother of Queen Caroline, the unfortunate wife of the Regent (later George IV). He served with the British army in the Peninsular War, and raised a corps to fight Napoleon in 1815. He was killed in the action at Quatre Bras, at the head of his small force of Brunswickers.

Colonel (Sir) Colin Campbell (1776–1847), promoted Major-General in 1825. He started his career by running away to sea, and had prolonged service abroad before reaching Waterloo.

Colonel Sir John Colborne (1778–1863), later General Lord Seaton (1839) was especially favoured by Sir John Moore in Spain where he commanded, as at Waterloo, the 52nd Foot.

General Miguel Ricardo de Alava (1771–1843), a Spanish soldier and diplomat who served under Wellington in Spain and later became a sort of military liaison diplomat representing his country in a succession of foreign assignments. He was in liaison with Wellington at Waterloo.

The size of the Prussian participation in the Waterloo campaign is shown by the gross estimated totals of troops, with 115,000 as the lowest figure and 140,000 as the highest. The actual standing complement of the Prussian Army of the Lower Rhine was 30,000; the 'parish' for this force was the area enclosed by the rivers Rhine, Meuse and Moselle. Taking a mean gross total of, say, 125,000 Prussians in the actions culminating in Waterloo, the extent of the concentration organised by Blücher can be appreciated.

Blücher, who is properly referred to as Prince Blücher of Wahlstadt, was 73 years of age in June, 1815. As mentioned earlier he was materially aided by Lt.-General Count von Gneisenau (1760–1831) who was Quarter-Master General and Chief of Staff. As his No. 3 there was Major-General von Grölmann, who was called Chief of the General Staff.

Just before Napoleon crossed the Belgian frontier Blücher was based with his H.Q. at Namur. He had disposed across the S.E. sector from Brussels, four army corps, each a self-contained entity. As a convenient yardstick it can be said that a corp represented approximately 25,000 men – and that was the figure Blücher agreed in advance to supply to Wellington in case of need. In the event, it was the 4th Corps that came in on the English left at Waterloo.

There is one most interesting Prussian absent from the list of Blücher's senior officers which follows. The omission needs explaining since most reference books state positively that he was at Waterloo. However, close reading of other works indicates that there may well have been a translator's error – there is a clear difference between 'He struggled against Napoleon', or 'He was in the struggle against Napoleon' and an embellishment claiming that he actually fought at Waterloo. The man concerned is General Karl von Clausewitz (1780–1831) who wrote, from his own experiences and arising out of a profound study of many military actions, a masterpiece text-book entitled *Vom Kriege*. Paradoxically, it was the defeated Napoleon who inspired this classic work which cold-bloodedly expounded military theories that were to dominate the 19th Century and much of the 20th. One of Clausewitz most quoted aphorisms is that War is the continuation of policy by other means.

Blücher's Army

1st Corps: Commanded by Lt.-General von Zieten. Senior officers of this corps were Major-Generals von Heinmetz, Pirch, Sagow, Count Henkel, von Roeder.

2nd Corps: Commanded by Major-General von Pirch. Senior officers of this corps were Major-Generals von Tippelskirch, Kraft, Brause, von Jurgas, and Colonels von Laugen and von Roehl.

3rd Corps: Commanded by Lt.-General von Thielmann. Senior officers of this corps were Major-Generals von Borcke, von Hobe, and Colonels von Luen, von Stulpnagel, von Mohnhaupt.

4th Corps: Commanded by General Count Friedrich Wilhelm von Bulow of Dennewitz (1755–1816). Senior officers of this corps were Lt.-General von Hake, Major-Generals von Ryssel, Losthin, and Colonel von Hiller.

In addition there was the Reserve Cavalry, commanded by General Prince Wilhelm of Prussia (who did not take part in the fighting).

(It may be noted that there are *two* senior officers in the above with the surname Pirch. It could seem reasonable to suppose they were relatives; but this is not necessarily so. Apparently, in their *military* context, the officer in the subordinate position in the 1st Corps was known as Pirch II; whilst his namesake in the 2nd Corps was known as Pirch I. Where there is room to distinguish (and really Pirch I attracts more attention as a Corps Commander) for the record:

Major-General Otto Karl Lorenz von Pirch was Pirch II (1st Corps)

Major-General George Dubislaw Ludwig Pirch was Pirch I (2nd Corps).

Here is now entered what might be called a Supplement to the earlier information on casualties, and certain other totals. In relation to the above, an earlier figure gives a Grand Total for Blücher's army of 123,172 (see p. 66 for break-down).

But what is really required (especially for a wargame situation) is what was the Prussian strength at Waterloo, i.e. at the actual battlefield when the Prussians arrived, late in the day, to make their critical intervention in the battle?

The answer is, apparently, a grand total of 51,944 men and 104 guns.

This total of troops is acceptable *only* if it is assumed (a) that barely 15,000 Prussian (and purely Prussian, not other German) troops were actually in the main fighting before the rout, and/or (b) the following totals include all those Prussians who arrived *en scene* when the Guard had been broken by the English and when the chief function of the Prussians was to press home the full nature of the defeat.

From a wargame viewpoint it is essential to absorb the full meaning of the following figures which are cited by Captain William Siborne who, frankly, does not seem to appreciate their significance.

As far as research for this book has been concerned, these are the *only* figures directly linked to the hour as well as the day of the action; and, consequently, in the following tabulation it is to be accepted that all figures relate to 18th June, 1815, and only at the battle of Waterloo (not any of the side issues):

Local Time
4.30 p.m.
16.30 hours Present, in action *part* of the Prussian 4th Corps
            Inf (from different brigades) *Cav*   *Art*
            5,881   2,720 1,143 men 64 guns
            6,162
            These totals augmented by

6 p.m.
18.00 hours The remainder of the infantry of the 4th Corps
            6,953

7 p.m.
19.00 hours Now include *part* of the 1st Corps
            2,582   1,670   274 men 16 guns
            6,851
            and then *part* of the 2nd Corps, as
            6,469   4,468   386 men 24 guns
Totals   41,283 *Inf*   8,858 1,803   104

This gives a grand total (which must include large numbers who between 4.30 p.m. and 7.30 p.m. became casualties) of 51,944 officers and men plus 104 guns.

The French Army

Now for the senior French officers, all under the supreme command of Napoleon. As explained in the *Note on Rank* (p. 60), many of Napoleon's generals were classified as marshals in his heyday; and some of the following officers were graded as marshals of France after Waterloo. The ranks and titles that follow are as listed at Waterloo. General (D) = General of Division; General (B) = General of Brigade.

1st Corps: Commanded by General (D) Count d'Erlon (see note on page 77). Under his command were Generals (D) Durutte and Jacquinot (of the cavalry), and Generals (B) Bourgeois, Quiot, Schmitz, Aulard,

Nognez, Grenier, Pegot, Brune and Gobrecht, and Bruno of the cavalry.

2nd Corps: Commanded by General (D) Count Reille. Under his command were Generals (D) Bachelu, Girard, Foy, Piré, and Generals (B) Husson, Campy, Bauduin, Soye, Plat, Ganthieu, Janim, Hubert, Wathieu and Prince Jerome.

3rd Corps: Commanded by General (D) Count Vandamme. Under his command were Generals (D) Berthezene, Le Fol, Domon, and Generals (B) Gengoult, Dupeyroux, Dufour, Lagarde, Billard, Corsin, Domanger and Vinot.

6th Corps: Commanded by Count Lobau. Under his command were Generals (D) Simmer, Jeannin, Teste, and Generals (B) Belaiu, Bony, Tromelin, Lafite, Penne.

The Army of the Moselle (the 4th Corps): Commanded by General (D) Gérard. Under his command were Generals (D) Pecheux, Vechery, Morin, and Generals (B) Home, Schaeffen, Le Capitaine, Desprez, Hulot, Toussaint, Vallin, Berruyer.

Cavalry

This was a combination of cavalry drawn from the Army of the North and the Army of the Moselle, under the overall command of Marshal Grouchy (see p. 67). He had four Corps:

1st Corps, Cavalry: Commanded by General (D) Pajol. Under his command were Generals (D) Soult, Subervic, and Generals (B) St. Laurent, Ormeil, Colbert, Merlin.

2nd Corps, Cavalry: Commanded by General (D) Excelmanns. Under his command were Generals (D) Strolz and Chastel, and Generals (B) Burthe, Montfalcon and Vincent.

3rd Corps, Cavalry: Commanded by General (D) Count Valmy. Under his command were Generals (D) Roussel d'Hurbal and L'Heriter, and Generals (B) Picquet, Guyton, Blancard and Donop.

4th Corps, Cavalry: Commanded by General (D)

Count Milhaud. Under his command were General (D) Wathieu, and Generals (B) Dubois, Travers, Dolost, Farine and Vial.

There is one conspicuous absentee from the above abstract of the Order of Battle: Marshal Michel Ney. It is difficult to appreciate quite what was in Napoleon's mind but it could well be that until about 13th June he himself was undecided. He, Napoleon, could chase first one army and then the other of his opponents. Or he could fight one battle himself and allot the other to one of his marshals – as he had done at Auerstadt and Jena on the same day in 1806.

His plan was fluid, open to resolution in the circumstances on the spot. Hence he delayed until the last minute before appointing Ney in general overall command of the French left and Grouchy as overall commander of the French right, with himself in the Centre over the overall commanders!

And in a manner which is quite beyond understanding or logical explanation he put Grouchy, a cavalryman, in command of what was really an infantry operation, and gave Ney, an infantryman, charge of what was in no small part a cavalry operation.

This was a major and catastrophic blunder made solely by Napoleon. One can emphasise 'solely' because there is evidence that Ney warned him of the British tenacity and fighting spirit, whilst the famous and veteran Marshal Soult (already beaten by Wellington in Spain and South France) advised him that victory would only come if he engaged in manoeuvre rather than in a slogging match, in any sort of pitched battle. All that was ignored, deliberately, by Napoleon.

As far as the wargame is concerned, it would make an interesting ploy to have Grouchy commanding the French left and Ney away out on the French right. The probability is that whatever the French did they were bound to lose so long as Napoleon entered into a headlong clash at a position which the extremely experienced

Wellington had chosen well in advance and had long prepared for, whereas his opponent was improvising all the time.

8
Terrain and Weather
◆◆◆◆

The countryside where the most decisive battle of the 19th Century was fought over is of such a generally gentle nature that a slight rise tends to be honoured by the name of hill and a shallow depression called a valley.

In the sense that it has not (so far) succumbed to urbanisation and building development, the scene where Napoleon was defeated by Wellington is much as it was in 1815 – a rolling landscape, like a long and slow swell on a great ocean. The scene carries no natural landmarks of note. Like most other places in Lower Flanders it is not photogenic. In a low key, it cannot be denied that the French moved from a shallow depression to attack, uphill and on a modest ridge, an Anglo-Dutch-Belgian force positioned there.

The setting for this great battle, so calmly reminiscent of a Paul Nash painting, so everyday, so unassuming, and so commonplace, is still such that a motorist moving along the modern Route N.5 southwards from Brussels to Charleroi, could transit the valley of the action, with no more than a glance left and right, in a couple of minutes. But for the man-made memorial mound on the West of the highway he would observe no more than an agreeable agricultural landscape with, notably, none of the medieval manorial hedges and ditches which persist in England.

Yet that was not what the experienced eye of the Allied military commander saw when in the summer of 1814 he had travelled by chance through this part of Flanders.

In a speech in the House of Lords to move a vote of thanks to the Duke of Wellington on his famous victory, Lord Bathurst said that it was a remarkable fact that in the preceding summer the Duke had noticed the defensive advantages of the ridge close to Waterloo village; and had then gone so far as to make a note of the topography, stating to his entourage that if it should fall to his lot to fight a battle in the area for the protection of Brussels, then he would endeavour to do so in that particular position.

This astonishing precognition of events is a factor ignored by, or unknown to, critics who later assessed the Duke as 'lucky'. However, detailed examination of the scene indicates clearly the 'eye for position' which Wellington undoubtedly possessed.

The centre point or main axis of the conflict area was the minute village of Waterloo which stood on the southernmost fringe of the Forest of Soignes.

The scene of the battle is thus 12 miles from Brussels and 18 miles from the next major town on this road, Charleroi, which is today a centre of coal-mining but which was made a fortified city in 1666 by the Spanish Governor Rodrigo who named it after the King of Spain.

The battlefield was in the open country astride the modern N.5 highway which bisects the scene of the conflict. The Forest of Soignes stood as a backcloth to the command point taken up by the Duke of Wellington on the northern ridge of the valley across which the French attacked.

Critics have said that this forest could have been a fatal trap to a retreating force if the Duke had been obliged to give way. This is unacceptable criticism: the forest was of tall beeches, passable for men but not for guns, so that with only a few regiments of resolute infantry, who could exploit this natural cover, any pursuers could easily have been held at bay.

In Fig. 4, or even in the detail of an Ordnance Survey large-scale map, the disposition of the various action points can be positively shown; but what may not be so readily apparent is that the low ridge on the Duke's side was high enough – and with sufficient angle of ascent approach when viewed from the trough of the valley – to give natural protection to troops artfully sited just over the crest of the skyline *as seen from below*.

This crest was sufficiently superior to the valley to give a commanding view of the whole panorama before Wellington. In contrast, the French (facing uphill) could hardly see anything more than the forward cannon and the screen of skirmishers.

Thus the position taken up by Wellington was splendid for defence, and almost as good for launching an attack downhill.

Incidentally, the Allied/British line faced overall just East of South. Thus as the great battle raged from noon to early evening the Sun came round more and more into French eyes, so that, in the final stages, the French extreme right was sun-down from Wellington's command point. For convenience, a token command point has been shown on Fig. 4, page 88, but in fact, of course, the Duke moved from place to place along the line throughout the action.

Let us now try to reconstruct the outlook from that command point, which was to the fore of Waterloo and just east of the hamlet of Mont Saint Jean, 2 miles distant.

The axis of the Allied line was orientated approximately ENE/WSW but nearer 77°/257° True. As C. in C., the Duke of Wellington was alert to all that was going on

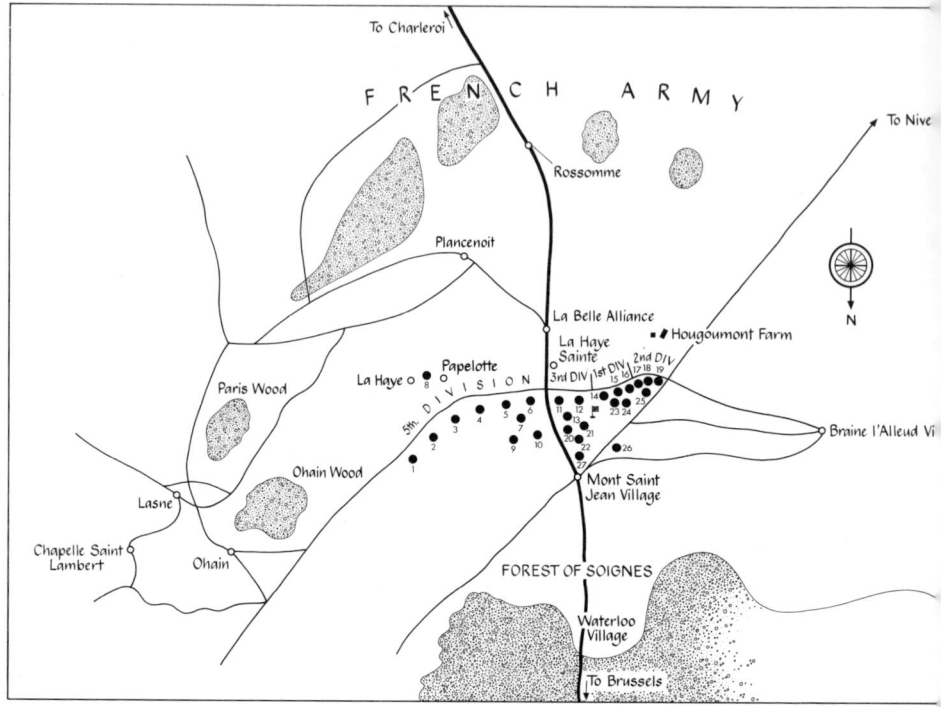

Fig. 4. Wellington's view of the battlefield.
   Key:

Flag: Duke of Wellington, Sir A. Gordon, ADC., Lord Hill, Lord Uxbridge, Prince of Orange. But note: The Duke's H.Q. was in fact highly mobile.
1. Hussey, 6th Cavalry Brigade (Hussars)
2. Vandeleur, 4th Cavalry Brigade (Light)
3. Von Vincke, 5th Hanoverian Infantry Brigade
4. Best, 4th Hanoverian Infantry Brigade
5. Bylandt, Dutch and Belgian Brigade
6. Kempt, 8th British Infantry Brigade
7. Pack, 9th British Infantry Brigade
8. Detachments from 1, 2, 3 and 4 at Papelotte and La Haye
9. Ponsonby's Dragoons
10. Ghigny's Dutch and Belgian Horse
11. Ompteda, Brigade of German Legion
12. Kielmansegge, Hanoverian Brigade
    Detachment from 11 and 12 at La Haye Sante

as seen from his mobile 'command post' on the back of his chestnut charger 'Copenhagen'. This horse was a noble and imperturbable beast which died in 1835, aged 27.

Across the valley, clearly visible by pocket telescope when the cannon smoke permitted, Napoleon sat on his white stallion 'Marengo', his chosen position just west of the Imperial Guard, by La Belle Alliance village.

Scanning the British front line from right to left, i.e. from west to east, Wellington had an appreciable ravine on the far flank – no enemy cavalry charge could 'turn his line' on that side where a token Dutch-Belgian force was positioned as safeguard.

From the Duke's control point, bearing SSW (225°)

---

13. Kruse, Nassau Brigade
14. Halkett, 5th British Brigade
15. Maitland, 1st British Infantry Brigade (Guards)
16. Byng, 2nd British Infantry Brigade (Guards)
17. Adam, 3rd British Infantry Brigade (Light)
18. Du Plat, 1st Brigade, King's German Legion
19. Baron Halkett, 3rd Hanoverian Brigade
20. Somerset, Household Cavalry Brigade
21. Von Arèntschild, 7th Cavalry Brigade
22. Netherlands Heavy Cavalry Brigade
23. Dörnberg, 3rd Cavalry Brigade (King's German Legion Light Dragoons)
24. Dörnberg, 3rd Cavalry Brigade (23rd British Light Dragoons)
25. Grant, 5th Cavalry Brigade (Hussars)
26. Corps of Brunswickers, Horse and Foot
27. Lambert, 10th British Infantry Brigade
At Hougoumont: 2 companies from 1st Guards, and one company each from 2nd and 3rd Guards, Hanoverian Riflemen, Detachment of Nassau Regiment.

and at a distance of 1½ miles (2.5 km.) was a farmhouse, sometimes aggrandised by the title of château, marked on maps as Hougoumont but known locally simply as 'Goumont'.

Almost due south from Wellington and only ¾-mile (1,200 metres) distant on the modern N.5 highway was the farmhouse of La Haye Sainte. And still on this road, but a further 1¼ miles (2,200 metres) was La Belle Alliance – incidentally in being long before the battle and hence only fortuitously named as regards the winning alliance.

Two miles further South was Rossomme; it was just north of Rossomme that Napoleon positioned the Imperial Guard astride the highway.

To the east of that Guard, and bearing 165° from Wellington, was the hamlet of Plancenoit, 2 miles (3,000 metres) away from him.

Bearing 120° were the houses at Papelotte, distant from him 1,650 yards (2,600 metres) and this spot adjoined La Haye, bearing 116° and not to be confused with La Haye Sainte on the highway.

Due east, in the direction from which the Prussians eventually appeared was Ohain Wood, and beyond that Lasne.

On the highway (the modern N.5) and 8 miles (12 km.) south of the Duke, beyond Genappe, was the key village of Quatre Bras (Four Arms cross-roads) leading eastwards to Sombreffe and Namur and westwards to Nivelles, both being out of sight. This minor road runs nearly straight for 26 miles N.W. to S.E. across open country.

A main engagement took place near Sombreffe, at Ligny by Fleurus. This latter was of course also out of sight of Wellington's position; it lay 8 miles (12 km.) N.E. of Charleroi on the modern N.21.

Figure 4 shows how the Duke would have viewed the scene to his south, and indicates the position that his various forces took up for action on 18th June. That is to say, the picture is not necessarily accurate for any time before 11.00 hours on that day because, earlier, some troops were still arriving, and some had gone further south, to Quatre Bras, from which they later withdrew.

The complementary map (Fig. 5, page 92) shows how the battlefield would be viewed by Napoleon who, because of his decision to split his own army, meant that he had to look N.E. towards the Prussians and North towards the Allies under Wellington. In his case the interesting point is that his army had been in progressive contraction from the moment it crossed the frontier. It had started on a front of 20+ miles (30+ km.), and it had, as it were, funnelled down to less than 3 miles (5 km.) facing the enemy front of effectively less than 2 miles (3 km.), and with the fiercest fighting on a front of barely 1,200 yards (1,100 m.).

Weather Reports for Charleroi District
Friday, 16th June, 1815
12.00 noon (12.00 hours): Clear blue sky. Visibility 12 miles. Line squall moving in from far south.
6 p.m. (18.00 hours): Rain; increasing to heavy rain.
7.30 p.m. (19.30 hours): Thunderstorm. Rain through the night, abates before dawn. Dark night, 10/10ths overcast.

Saturday, 17th June, 1815
12.00 noon (12.00 hours): Close, high humidity, intensely hot. Heavy cloud in the west, moving east.
3 p.m. (15.00 hours): Thunderstorm with downpour. Ground turned into a quagmire. Black mud covered uniforms and faces.
6 p.m. (18.00 hours): Storm breaks up. Patches of showers. Heat mists rise over low ground.
8.30 p.m. (20.30 hours): Pouring rain through most of the night, to dawn. Overcast 10/10ths. Very dark night.

Sunday, 18th June, 1815
8 a.m. (08.00 hours): Rain has stopped. Temperature drops appreciably.

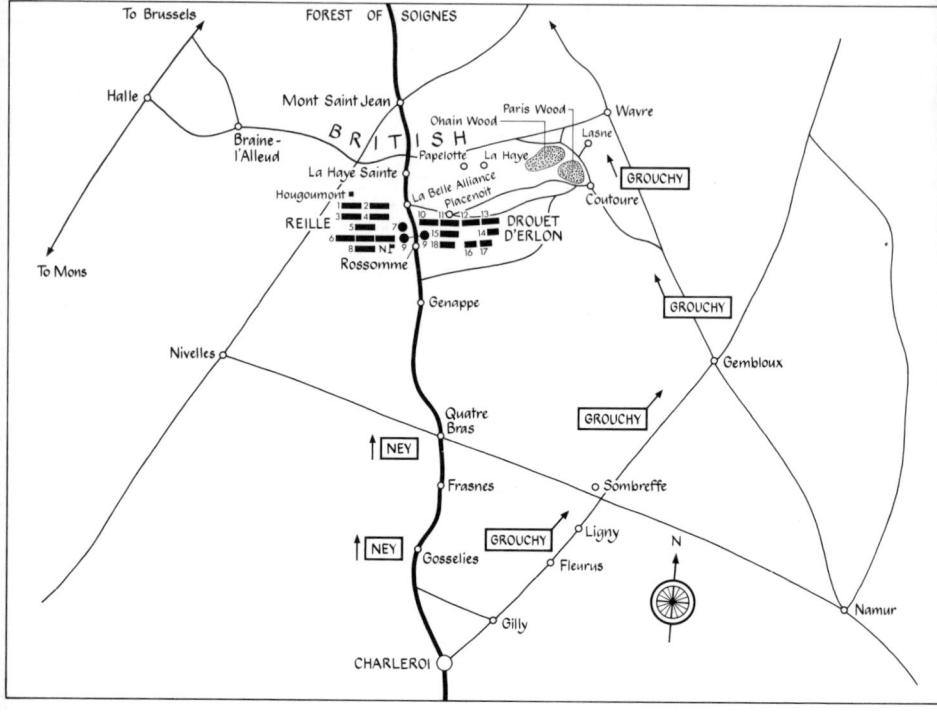

Fig. 5. How Napoleon saw the battlefield. On 14th June, Ney had been given command of the advance on the left and Grouchy the advance on the right. The aim at that time was to crush the Prussians first and then overwhelm the British and allied force.

Key:
- 1–4. The three infantry divisions of Reille's Second Corps, under their commanders, Bachelu, Jerome Bonaparte and Foy.
- 5. Reille's cavalry division, commanded by Piré.
- 6. Kellermann's Third Cavalry Corps (2 divisions).
- 7. Lobau's Sixth Corps (3 divisions), subsequently moved to the right flank very late in the day to engage the Prussians.
- 8. Guyot and the Heavy Cavalry of the Imperial Guard.

8.30 a.m. (08.30 hours): Clouds clearing rapidly. Sun breaks through.
10.30 a.m. (10.30 hours): Clear sky, sunshine. Very muddy, ground soaked and drying slowly.
11 a.m. (11.00 hours) onwards: Clear sky, but visibility partly obscured by rising heat mist, partly by dense clouds of smoke in the periods of cannonades.
9 p.m. (21.00 hours): Clear sky. Moonlight.

9–9. Partly behind Lobau (7) and astride the Charleroi-Brussels road was the Imperial Guard. Napoleon had his command and observation posts behind and to the left of the Guard.
10–13. The four infantry divisions of Drouet D'Erlon's First Corps commanded by Durette (10), Marcognet (11), Allix (12) and Donzelot (13).
14. D'Erlon's cavalry division, commanded by Jacquinot.
15. Milhaud's Fourth Cavalry Corps (2 divisions).
16. Infantry of Lobau's Sixth Corps, after their move to right flank.
17. Cavalry divisions of Subervie and Domon (detached from Grouchy's forces).
18. Light Cavalry of Imperial Guard, commanded by Lefebvre-Desnouettes.

9
Preliminary Moves
⟡⟡⟡

Wednesday, 14th June, 1815
Learning of French moves, Blücher did not hesitate: he ordered his 1st Corps to make a tactical withdrawal through Charleroi, and his 2nd, 3rd and 4th Corps to converge on his H.Q. These forces were in the vicinity of the towns of Dinant, Liège, Namur. The point for concentration was Sombreffe, W.N.W. of Namur.

As at late afternoon, 14th June, the Prussians were pouring into positions in the zone of the left (northern) bank of the R. Sambre, along the villages of Fleurus, Ligny, Sombreffe, Gembloux.

In parallel, but later (for reasons explained), in Brussels the first information report from General Zieten was received by Wellington. The Duke was baffled by Napoleon's move, but he ordered a brigade to move southwards on to Quatre Bras which more and more loomed on the map as a key cross-roads.

(Reminder: Check with Weather Report. Rain could make secondary roads impassable for heavy cannon, supply wagons, etc.)

The importance of Quatre Bras is frequently overlooked, for this is its true significance:

When Napoleon decided to move on the Prussians first, he knew that Blücher and Wellington had agreed, in advance, that the one should and would go to the aid of the other. Hence, in honour bound Wellington would have to move towards Blücher's force, i.e. S.E. from Brussels, passing through Quatre Bras. To forestall that, or at least make it exceedingly difficult, Napoleon had to detach from his total army some 40,000 troops from his left flank for use against the expected arrival of the British. Hence, there were 40,000 fewer against the Prussians who were to be his first objective. And it was because of that fact that Blücher had a numerical superiority of some 12,000 over the French in the battle about to develop at Ligny.

That which followed the opening moves of this gigantic action has all the elements of the knock-about in an all-in wrestling tag match, with, against all the rules, one contestant fighting at the same time two who are paradoxically separate yet together. This makes the narrative somewhat confusing because at any one time at least two actions, widely dispersed, are in progress.

It can help, certainly in a wargame, to get behind the thinking of the two opposing Commanders at Waterloo. Not being unkind, there was not really much thinking behind the actions of Blücher and the Prussians: all he and they wanted was to 'bash the French to pieces' as some slight repayment for the French victory against them nine years previously.

The very experienced Duke of Wellington, however, was deeply wary that the French movements reported due south of Brussels in the Charleroi area might well be feints to lure him away from the capital – and thus clear the route for Napoleon to advance from Mons.

The fact is that from the intelligence reports to his hand at this time (14th June) he could only 'place' one-sixth of the entire French army as actually with Napoleon in the Charleroi area.

In the past, Napoleon had secured sensational victories because of amazing forced marches which had brought his army to where it had been calculated by his adversary that it could not possibly be.

Thus, the vital question was whether, once again, Napoleon was staging a *coup* – huffing and puffing around Charleroi whilst rushing up a 'hidden' army on the Mons or even Lille approach.

The Duke wanted two things: (1) to have Napoleon irrevocably committed to action, and (2) for that action to be to the south of the Forest of Soignes on the site which gave him at least three aces out of four.

Against all that, Napoleon's angle was that he could achieve a major *coup* (politically, internationally) if only he could occupy Brussels which was the key to the whole of the Low Countries. The prize was enormous – the risk would be far reduced if he manoeuvred to take on Blücher first and then deal with the numerically far inferior Wellington.

The order was important. In his estimate, Blücher (aged 73) was far less formidable than Wellington (aged 46). By attacking the Prussians that action might well lure Wellington far clear of Brussels.

It can be accepted that Napoleon fed rumours into Brussels itself that he intended to advance on that city via Mons – such rumours would tend to hold Wellington back from any link-up with Blücher. But in fact his objective was to drive a wedge between the two opposing armies; the Prussians seemed to him ripe for plucking.

Nevertheless, it is important to note that at the time he reached Charleroi he had not finalised his plans beyond a decision to take on one of his opponents and then the other. In fact, even at this late stage, it seems he had not definitely decided on which of his gallant subordinates should do what.

All this, then, was as a prelude to what in effect was a real-life version of the philosopher's problem, viz. What would happen if an Irresistible Force met an Immovable Body?

The answer was provided at the battle of Waterloo – that there would occur an Unprecedented Event!

Curtain Raiser
Thursday, 15th June, 1815

The disposition of the French army after crossing the Belgian frontier was in three blocks or columns. The extreme left formation occupied Thuin. The middle column moved on Charleroi and continued N.E. to Fleurus, Napoleon being with this central force. On the right, the French formation moved towards the bridge at Chatelet, an isolated habitation south of the R. Sambre.

The opposition so far had amounted to no more than pin-pricks from the Prussian troops under General Zieten, and these were withdrawing in good order, and to plan.

The scope of the next day's operations was now decided. In principle the French commander decided that he would hold off or even beat back the Allied troops opposite his left wing, and, especially, thwart any moves by those Allies for a link-up with the Prussians.

The command of this wing was given to Marshal Ney – and there is a mystery about this. It was not until late on the night of Sunday, 11th June, that Ney, in Paris, was summoned to quit the capital and take part in the campaign in Flanders.

No explanation of this last-minute appointment has been made: it could be that Napoleon had deliberately left his trusted lieutenant in Paris to deal with any possible uprising against his return as Emperor and the reversion to the war conditions that had plagued Europe for 20 years.

However, Ney acted on the instant, and hardly had he arrived than he was directed to advance on Quatre Bras as soon as possible.

This instruction Ney acted on immediately. By 10 p.m. (22.00 hours) that night, Thursday, 15th June, troops under his command had occupied Gosselies and

Frasnes, the latter being 8 miles (12 km.) North of Charleroi and barely 3 miles short of Quatre Bras.

The French troops of this, the left wing, were now physically exhausted after hours of non-stop marching interspersed with running fights against the Prussians under Zieten. They had also had to winkle out Belgians, small in number but fighting desperately for their homes and property since 10 a.m. (10.00 hours).

Thus Ney was obliged to pause for his troops to recover their energy, for men and animals to be fed and watered, and, incidentally, for Ney to take stock of and reorganise as necessary the army he had so far hardly seen.

That done, albeit in skimped fashion, Ney rode back to Charleroi which he reached after midnight. He had been summoned for a meal and a conference with Napoleon.

Night of 15th/16th June
The midnight conference and dinner lasted until 2 a.m. (02.00 hours) and in full understanding of the position (as he supposed), Ney then rode back to Frasnes, which he reached about 03.00 hours.

He then: (1) Studied situation and intelligence reports.
(2) Studied the special maps prepared by the divisional commanders.
(3) Gave orders that he would meet all his subordinate commanders shortly after daybreak.
(4) Took some very necessary sleep.

The records show that at the time Ney put his head down to sleep he did not even know the names of many of the senior officers under his command.

Through the long day of 15th June Wellington had been on tenterhooks. Positive news that the French had taken Charleroi did not reach him until 3 p.m. (15.00 hours). He was most apprehensive, fearing that the

French move was selling him a dummy – and that Napoleon would still really come via the Mons road.

True, he despatched some troops southwards towards Quatre Bras; but as late as 10 p.m. (22.00 hours) on 15th June, he ordered more troops to leave for Quatre Bras and at the same time other troops to proceed to Ath on the Mons road.

In the late afternoon of this day of suspense a message came from the Duchess of Richmond to enquire whether, in the circumstances of which rumour had reached her, it would be best for her to cancel the Ball which she was giving that night in Brussels.

The danger of such an act was immediately apparent to the Duke in view of her connections and actual relationships with English and French interests most against Napoleon. Thus, the husband of the Duchess was the 4th Duke of Richmond and Lennox, and son of the 2nd Duke. His grandfather was one of the illegitimate sons of Charles II by Louise de Keroualle, a Frenchwoman who was made Duchess of Portsmouth in 1673 and given a French title by Louis XIV (*Le Roi Soleil*) in 1674. The present (1815) Duke was a tremendous swell, who had the honour of fighting a duel against the preposterous Frederick Augustus, Duke of York and Albany, of parody fame. It was convenient for the Richmonds to reside in Brussels at this time, and, in fact, he held the rank of General in the British Army. The Ball was the high social event of the season, and Wellington rightly argued that cancellation would feed rumour, and rumour would foster panic. It would spread the notion that Napoleon would reach and occupy Brussels – and such an idea would be disastrous for morale among the apprehensive Dutch and Belgian forces who knew only too well what occupation by a French army would really mean.

To forestall any such rumours and misgivings, the Duke put on a bold and nonchalant front, openly displaying the *sang froid habituel* for which the English were famous.

Ostentatiously he caused the Duchess to be informed that he saw no reason why he should not attend her ball, accompanied by his A.D.C. and staff.

That message being despatched and publicised by word-of-mouth he gave orders for further troops to be moved southwards on the Charleroi road. Meanwhile he made a confidential communiqué to his corps commanders and other senior officers that they were *required* to put in appearance at the Ball, there socialise and circulate; and then at discretion and by individual excuse they were to slip away from the jollity and join their troops moving off southwards to their date with destiny.

That, then, was the position regarding the Duke and his staff in Brussels as Napoleon was conferring with Ney in Charleroi. At 3 a.m. (03.00 hours) the Duke was still at the Ball, and observed to be 'very cheerful'. But at 5 a.m. (05.00 hours) he was riding southwards in all haste, heading for Quatre Bras and accompanied by the Prussian liaison officer, Baron von Müffling.

Before departing Brussels, Müffling had sent an express messenger racing to Blücher to say that Wellington was leaving at about dawn to ride to Quatre Bras with the intention of having a meeting with Blücher, so that the two commanders could have an *ad hoc* conference in the field as to how to bring about a decisive battle with the French. Müffling stated further that Wellington was in a mind to bring his whole Allied force to supplement the Prussians in their concentration near Sombreffe, but that the Duke desired to have details of what was to be agreed to be made at first hand.

On receipt of that message Blücher at once saw the point, and, with his staff, moved from the area of Ligny cross-country towards Quatre Bras. The two commanders in fact met by the windmill at Bry. Wellington and Müffling reached Quatre Bras at 11.15 a.m. (11.15 hours) and rode eastwards to their rendezvous 15 minutes later. At noon, by Bry, the Duke (who could at times be blunt) asked Blücher (with his right hand man, General Gneisenau) what they wished him to do.

A rapid Appreciation of the Prussian situation was given to the Duke. In summary form, Blücher had a grand total of 80,000 troops who were disposed in the main along a chain of low hills that overlooked land from Ligny to Sombreffe, on the left bank of the R. Sambre. There were some troops in all the villages and farms below the main line in the hills from which, in the distance, the vanguard of the advancing French troops had been sighted.

Wellington, who did not speak German, informed Müffling for Blücher's ears that as soon as his army had concentrated at or near Quatre Bras he was prepared to thrust forwards and southwards on to Frasnes and then Gosselies, to cut the French forces in their rear, severing their line to Charleroi and Paris beyond.

This plan was not acceptable to Blücher, who requested that Wellington should bring his army from Quatre Bras through Sombreffe to Namur, thus forming a Reserve behind the front rank Prussians.

To this Wellington gave limited concurrence (because, though he did not say so, such a move would take him even further from the Mons–Brussels road). He said he would follow Blücher's request *provided he himself was not being attacked.*

That exchange took place at about 2 p.m. (14.00 hours) Friday, 16th June, and at almost exactly that time the French were attacking at Quatre Bras, a happening of which Wellington was then ignorant.

Whilst (above) we have accounted for the forenoon and early afternoon of the Duke and Blücher, the French under Ney had had their stand-easy and were being lined up for battle.

Napoleon had given orders to secure the left wing by attacking at Quatre Bras, and for this purpose Ney had been allotted 40,000 troops which included the formidable cuirassiers under Kellermann and the equally terrible lancers under Piré. The allocation of 40,000 included the 1st corps commanded by Drouet d'Erlon, plus the 2nd corps under Reille, plus the cavalry division of Lefebvre-Desnouettes.

Ney's reconnaissance cavalry convinced him that the Allied opposition was no match for his forces as he spent the forenoon drawing up the battle orders . . . *but hardly had he made his plan with his commanders than peremptory orders came from Napoleon direct ordering the whole of the 1st corps under Drouet d'Erlon to leave Ney and march eastwards to join Napoleon at the attack on Ligny!*

That was the sort of order not even Ney could disobey, and, consequently, before he even began his attack, which Napoleon had himself ordered, Ney permitted Drouet d'Erlon to depart whilst he revised his battle plan.

So, at 2 p.m./3 p.m. (14.00/15.00 hours) on Friday, 16th June, anyone looking down on the battlefield would have observed a fantastic situation:

Napoleon was coming up on Ligny, nearly there . . .

Blücher's Prussians were at Ligny, facing the oncoming French . . .

Ney was coming on to Quatre Bras . . .

English troops were coming to Quatre Bras . . .

Dutch and Belgian troops (under the Prince of Orange) were at Quatre Bras.

And, most bizarre of all, Wellington himself, with his small escort/entourage, was in the open country between Quatre Bras and Ligny whilst just to the south of him a whole French corps under Drouet d'Erlon moved eastwards on a parallel course and quite unaware that a prize beyond belief was just over the hill and there for the capturing!

A spotlight on the Dutch-Belgian force at Quatre Bras at this hour and date: The Prince of Orange had under command no more than 7,000 infantry from Flanders, plus one English battalion plus one battalion of horse artillery. Obviously, at best this force could offer but a holding action against Ney (even with his depleted forces).

Quatre Bras (Four Arms) was, literally, the crossroads – intersection of the modern N.5 and N.49, extending from Nivelles in the west to Namur in the east.

In 1815, on the west side of Quatre Bras was the Bois de Bossu, the Hunchback Wood. On slightly higher level ground, overlooking the junction, was a farmhouse named Gemiancourt. To the east were enclosed fields of the hamlet of Pierremont.

Action is about to begin here at Quatre Bras and at the same time at Ligny barely 10 miles to the S.E.

10
Quatre Bras and Ligny
◇◆◇◆◇◆◇

Friday afternoon, and early evening, 16th June, 1815
Two major actions are now taking place simultaneously; and neither commander knows clearly what is happening to the other. It almost appears, in retrospect, like some monstrous and macabre ballet as the massed legions of soldiers in their gay and gaudy uniforms advance and retreat, swaying to and fro in a surrealist struggle as rainstorms and thunder accompany the different Corps in this tragedy for so many of the 'bit players'.

But first, if it were not too real in the frequent muddle of war, an element of comedy comes into the movement of the 1st Corps of Drouet d'Erlon. It will be recalled that before Ney began his attack on Quatre Bras (an event about to be described) Napoleon had withdrawn the 1st Corps which was ordered to march eastwards to the battle at Ligny. Nobly, if with mystification, this force moved from Quatre Bras; it had hardly gone halfway to Ligny when a messenger came at full gallop from Ney to say that later orders from Napoleon had placed full command in Ney's hands, and now Ney demanded that Drouet d'Erlon turn right about and come back to Quatre Bras!

Obedient to this summons, the 1st Corps, making an about turn, now started to march on Quatre Bras (where they could have done a great deal of damage). However, just as they were getting into their stride, moving westwards, another messenger arrived, with a demand from Napoleon to know why the devil the 1st Corps is delaying arrival at Ligny where it is badly needed?

So, once again, the unhappy 1st Corps had to about turn, and head for Ligny. In short and in sum, the 1st Corps marched and counter-marched all day long between Ligny and Quatre Bras without firing a shot in either battle.

This extraordinary episode accordingly does not affect the main narrative to which a return is now made – to Quatre Bras with Ney on the offensive at about 2.30 p.m. (14.30 hours).

At about 8 a.m. (08.00 hours) in the morning of the 16th, apparently making a record or a kind of log of the decisions and discussions that had taken place at the midnight rendezvous so shortly before, Napoleon wrote to Ney to say that his general plan was to divide the army into two wings and a reserve, the reserve to be brought into action on either wing as circumstances arose or chance offered.

Furthermore, Napoleon declared in writing that he would commit himself to a decisive battle only on that wing into which he had ordered the reserve – it being the duty of Ney to interpret this as situations arose, for the uncommitted wing was to be regarded as a holding action only.

Thus, according to agreed plan, Ney ordered his wing to advance on Quatre Bras; but he had already been 'milked' of Drouet d'Erlon's division, as already described. So, at about 2.30 p.m. (14.30 hours) a major French assault was mounted on the cross-roads area where, as Wellington had discovered a few hours earlier, there were some 7,800 troops under the Prince of Orange.

The French took by storm the farm named Gemiancourt, and then the farm buildings and cottages at Pierremont. Advance units had occupied the southern side of Hunchback Wood (Bois de Bossu); and the artillery was delivering an increasingly heavy fire from the slightly higher ground by the cross-roads.

It was clear that against a considerably superior and aggressive French force the Dutch and Belgians would not long hold out. But just as they were on the point of wavering, surprise support came from the west, from the Nivelles direction, in the shape of the 5th British Division commanded by Sir Thomas Picton, accompanied by the Duke of Brunswick's corps. That was at about 3 p.m. (15.00 hours); and from then onwards until the late evening more and more English troops came on the scene, down the N.5 highway from Brussels.

A furious battle now developed. The Dutch and Belgian cavalry moved into action, and was accompanied by the Brunswick cavalry whose leader, the gallant Duke himself, was unfortunately killed. However, the Dutch and Belgian infantry, which had been wavering, now took heart alongside the English and Hanoverians who (in the words of Siborne) were fighting like demons.

Locked in battle, the French artillery and cavalry was unable to break the brigades of Kempt and Pack under Picton's command.

(Note here the lesson: that the infantry could beat artillery and cavalry – it is the key to the follow-up battle at Waterloo.)

However, there was some really savage action which, curiously enough, only further inflamed those fighting the French.

About 4 p.m. (16.00 hours) Ney received a message from Napoleon who was attacking the Prussians at Ligny, to the east. Napoleon's message was *written* at 2 p.m. (14.00 hours) and it ordered Ney to make a full-scale attack on Quatre Bras.

Ney read this message, and married it up with the information he had that Drouet d'Erlon's corps was marching back towards him (see above).

Putting the two facts together, Ney decided to wait for Drouet d'Erlon's corps to join him and thus give him overwhelming superiority.

Parallel in time (and partly geographically) Wellington was returning from his meeting with Blücher. With fresh English troops arriving all the time, and with the forces already in battle holding their own, the Duke directed every available man into action immediately on arrival . . . and this continual inflow occurred exactly when Ney was waiting that vital half-hour for Drouet d'Erlon to come in from the east.

In fact, Drouet d'Erlon's column was *within sight of* Quatre Bras when the peremptory order from Napoleon previously referred to, ordered an about turn *away from Quatre Bras.*

With his spy-glass Ney observed the turn-round with amazement and anger (and probably sent an A.D.C. at the gallop to ask what the hell was going on).

Unabated, the fight raged on; then, at about 5 p.m. (17.00 hours) Ney received a further message from Napoleon – a message written at 3.15 p.m. (15.15 hours). This, in the best flamboyant French style, declared that the 'Fate of France' was in the hands of Ney.

This message was taken by Ney *au pied de la lettre,* that is to say, exactly as it read. Napoleon, his commander, had ordered (earlier) an all-out attack on Quatre Bras, and now, it seems, there was that vital and critical climax in the battle(s) against the enemy which required Ney to rise as the Supreme Saviour of La France *et cetera* and *et cetera.*

Consequently, reading the situation to be that *everything* depended on him at Quatre Bras, and with a completely blind spot that Napoleon might be relying on the arrival of Drouet d'Erlon from the west, Ney now issued a direct order for Drouet d'Erlon to turn about and at once join him at Quatre Bras! And that was what Drouet did, even though he was within sight of the French at Ligny . . . where, at 6 p.m. (18.00 hours) the French had imagined the advancing army coming in from the west to be Allied troops marching to aid Blücher!

In these incredible circumstances, Drouet did not finally link up with Ney until night had fallen.

Meanwhile, at Quatre Bras at about 6.30 p.m. (18.30 hours) the English Guards had arrived, stiffening the troops already there and now slightly outnumbering Ney's forces. And there were more troops on the way. . . .

First, Hunchback Wood was re-occupied. Then the French were forced from Pierremont, and as night came down the main enemy force had fallen right back on to Frasnes village though a pocket of resistance held out at Gemiancourt.

Wellington decided this must be taken at once, and ordered a full-scale assault which was successful just as night closed in.

The position now, as regards the French left wing, was that Ney was right back where he started when Napoleon had ordered him to advance on and take Quatre Bras in a holding operation. The Allied losses amounted to some 4,700 killed or wounded, and the French total was about 4,300.

On this sector, both armies had fought grimly for hours on end. From Ney's viewpoint he had to wait for Drouet d'Erlon's corps to come in from the east; he had to re-form his army; and he had to rest, feed and revive his soldiers. That would occupy him most of the night of 16th/17th June.

Ligny

Now to turn back the clock and study the parallel action of Napoleon, with Marshal Grouchy starting the attack on the Prussians at Ligny at about 3 p.m. (15.00 hours) 16th June, Friday afternoon and on to full darkness at 9 p.m. (21.00 hours).

The French did not rate the Prussian opposition

highly. Unquestionably, Napoleon here made the fatal mistake of underestimating the enemy. However, when the battle was engaged, and when it was not the walk-over he had more than half expected, he strove to remedy this by calling in the corps of Drouet d'Erlon (as described above) from Ney, at the same time summoning 10,000 troops of Lobau's 6th Corps to come quickly from Charleroi, which was 8 miles (12 km.) distant.

Consequently, when by skilful direction in the battle a Prussian reverse was achieved in the centre, near Ligny village, Napoleon was completely unable to exploit the advantage as it should have been. There was no help from Drouet . . . Ney did not swing round and envelop the Prussian right – and as for Lobau, he quite simply arrived too late.

Hence, after $5\frac{1}{2}$ hours of battle the Prussian army was defeated *on the battlefield* but it was not annihilated. On the contrary, the major part of the Prussian force at Ligny escaped northwards through the night; and since the 4th Corps of von Bülow had not been able to get anywhere near to Ligny though it was coming rapidly westwards from Liège, Blücher was able to order a concentration at Wavre (1) partly from those retreating from Ligny and (2) partly from von Bülow's corps.

The turning point at Ligny took place at about 6 p.m. (18.00 hours) when the French left halted its advance and re-formed to face a threatened attack coming in from the west i.e. Drouet d'Erlon's to-and-fro division which was mistaken for enemy forces! As shown above, Ney had ordered the mysterious force to turn back east, and so the French left flank at Ligny now turned to resume action and deal with a major thrust by Blücher's Guards. This attack really spent the Prussian effort, but just when the French might well (had they had Drouet d'Erlon with them) have moved in and mopped up all opposition, down came a terrible rainstorm accompanied by thunder and lightning. In this frantic confusion the Prussian army melted away, escaping destruction by a miracle, and preparing almost at once to resume fighting. But not that night: Blücher was able to declare that his army had lost the day but not its honour. And, in fact, more than ever were the Prussians determined eventually to defeat the French in a final victory – and to that end there was nothing that Blücher would not do for his ally Wellington.

As for the Duke, who had made up his mind to make an all-out attack on Ney's force as soon as dawn broke the next day, he heard with deep concern of Blücher's defeat at Ligny in the west. This news reached him about 9 p.m. (21.00 hours). The messenger reported on the battle at Ligny, of the forces Blücher still had under control, and especially of the high *morale* with which the Prussians were imbued as they made their withdrawal to Wavre.

What should Wellington now do? It was now no longer a question of cutting off Napoleon by an advance on Charleroi – on the contrary, the sensible thing to do would be to withdraw northwards, towards Brussels, and halt to resume the fight at a point of latitude coincident with that at Wavre.

The Duke must have smiled inwardly at the action now being forced upon him, since the site at Mont Saint Jean, which he had noticed, noted and commented upon to his entourage the previous Summer, was exactly level with Wavre, from which it was distant a bare 8 miles (12 km.). Paradoxically, the set-back at Ligny and the confrontation at Quatre Bras had combined to bring the Allies and the Prussians geographically closer together, and had thus complicated and confused French plans.

Consequently, Wellington sent back Blücher's messenger with this reply: that he would withdraw to Mont Saint Jean, and there he would halt and fight a general battle with the French if Blücher would guarantee to send him a single corps of 25,000 troops.

Even before the answer came – and it was to be a very positive affirmative – Wellington set in motion the wholesale withdrawal of the Allied troops at Quatre

Bras. And that went on all through the stormy and dark night.

The narrative may justifiably be interrupted here to point out the astounding endurance of the Duke who really showed himself a man of iron – though the nickname Iron Duke only came into use 25 years later (as explained in the Appendix). Thus, from the progress set out above, he had been on duty in Brussels from at least 9 p.m. on Thursday, 15th June, before he went to the Duchess of Richmond's Ball, which he left at 3 a.m. on the morning that he rode to Quatre Bras, then rode to meet Blücher, then rode back to Quatre Bras to defeat Ney's force, and now he was directing the withdrawal to Mont Saint Jean! Perhaps he had the ability to sleep or cat-nap in the saddle, but, demonstrably, by Saturday, 16th June at 11 p.m. (23.00 hours) he had been on the go for at least 26 hours non-stop.

Reprise

Saturday, 17th June, 1815

The furious storm of the night had considerably abated by dawn, and at 8 a.m. (08.00 hours) Napoleon could make a reckoning after a new situation report had been digested. News was despatched to Paris of a great victory at Ligny where some 12,000 Prussians had been killed or wounded. It was not necessary to mention that the French had lost 10,000 but guarded reference could be made of wholesale desertions from the enemy's ranks amounting to a total of perhaps as many as 8,000 troops.

In fact, on the left bank of the R. Sambre, from Ligny to Sombreffe, the Prussian army had vanished northwards. Convinced that it was now nothing more than a disordered rabble, Napoleon saw no real reason to hasten to cut the remnants to pieces. A senior cavalry officer had reported to him that the Prussians were in full retreat on Liège and Namur – which meant that they would have no chance or hope of re-forming and joining up with Wellington.

In fact, Napoleon was misinformed. Blücher himself, wounded and nearly lost as he made his get-away in the dark and blustery night, was fortunate in having the coldly professional competency of his senior staff officer, Gneisenau, to shepherd the defeated army northwards to union with von Bülow in the Wavre area.

Clearly, Napoleon now saw, he would next have to take on the Allied forces under Wellington. He needed time to re-form his forces for this, and, consequently, instead of pressing home the advantage gained on the right wing he spent the whole of the forenoon of Saturday, 17th June, with his army at Ligny. This may well have been beneficial in giving them time to reorganise, re-victual, replenish stores and ammunition, and generally have a stand easy after a grim day – before the final struggle so near ahead.

It is also hinted in prissy and bowdlerized terms that Napoleon himself took things easy this morning because he had an awkward complaint that had not permitted him to sleep. In fact he had had a bad attack of that 'distressing and universal complaint' which the physicians term haemorrhoids and the vulgar term piles. This painful affliction has been put forward to account for his lack of initiative throughout the forenoon of the 17th, but, though the illness was undoubtedly true, the real reason for delay was his attempt to solve the mystery as to where the English would stand and fight – or rather where they could be cornered and forced to stand and fight.

He had been annoyed by the shuttle-cock movements of Drouet d'Erlon; but now, when he received a dawn situation report sent by Ney at 5 a.m. (05.00 hours) and received by Napoleon before 7 a.m. (07.00 hours), he realised that he had been handed a hidden ace in that Drouet d'Erlon's whole corps was fresh and without casualties.

He now despatched indefinite, imprecise, and largely

incomprehensible orders, which Ney received at 9 a.m. (09.00 hours), telling his trusted lieutenant that he must inform him, Napoleon, of whatever took place in front of his army, and that he must (if possible but not otherwise or further) take up position at Quatre Bras.

Ney, baffled by this woolly directive, continued to reorganise, re-form and replenish his entire left wing, all far south of Quatre Bras, which position the tail end of the Allied forces was thus permitted to evacuate unimpeded. In fact, Wellington had had by 7.30 a.m. (07.30 hours) full details of the defeat at Ligny; and thus whilst Ney and Napoleon were dallying he was able to secure invaluable time for an organised withdrawal, details of which were communicated to Blücher far away on the Allied left.

Of course, Allied troops were, at this time, still leaving Brussels for Quatre Bras; orders were sent to them to stop short on the ridge on the edge of the Forest of Soignes, near Waterloo village where the Duke would set up his H.Q.

At about the same time, Napoleon had now made up his mind and his plan. First, just to make sure of the Prussians, he gave orders for Marshal Grouchy to pursue the beaten Blücher northwards to Wavre, whence he could converge on Brussels in due course. The main objective for Grouchy was to prevent any force moving westwards to join the British at Quatre Bras (which, in fact, they were already abandoning in full withdrawal). Grouchy took off 30,000 troops. . . .

Secondly, at 11 a.m. (11.00 hours) Napoleon gave orders for the 6th Corps under Lobau (the corps which had arrived late at Ligny) and the Imperial Guard to march on Quatre Bras, to which he himself was proceeding. The order was given at about the time when most of the British had left the area – but to cover the infantry and artillery withdrawal Wellington had given the Earl of Uxbridge a more or less free hand to use his cavalry squadrons.

Thus it was that when Napoleon reached Quatre

Bras, at around 2 p.m. (14.00 hours), like Old Mother Hubbard he found the cupboard bare. Nowhere could he find Ney's troops with whom he had expected to rendezvous; and as the ghastly facts sank in, as he realised that in an imperial bungle both he and Ney separately and collectively had allowed the English to escape from a trap that very morning, Napoleon was very bitter. In anguish he exclaimed: *'On a perdu la France!'*

However, snapping out of inaction he realised there was just a chance of catching the rear guard. Sending word for Ney to come at once, Napoleon himself took charge of the pursuit of the retreating Allied forces. He might, possibly, have had some success in this action had not, at the critical moment, a thunderstorm with torrents of rain descended from angry skies. With the soil turned into gooey cloying mud the pursuers were confined to the hard-standing of the highway along which the pursued were moving, and thus the casualties were of no more than a trivial total with the main bulk of the Allied forces safely back at the latitude of Mont Saint Jean by 6.30 p.m. (18.00 hours).

Only four days off the Summer solstice, there was full daylight as the British and Allied forces took up defence positions as the rain blessedly stopped. For two full hours there was no rain, and no possibility of any French attack as the Duke's army moved into their front line and second line positions. Then, as though to shield them further, the rain re-commenced just after 8.30 p.m. (20.30 hours) as the evening faded and the night came down. It rained and rained and rained for several hours, but by first light it had stopped.

At 2 a.m. (02.00 hours) on Sunday, 18th June, Wellington received at his H.Q. the message for which he had been waiting. This, from Blücher, was to say that the Prussian 4th Corps, commanded by General von Bülow, would move westwards from Wavre at dawn, to join the British and Allies as soon as possible.

This news was highly gratifying to the Duke, but he

did not at the time appreciate what sacrifice the Prussians were really making; nor has the run-of-the-mill historical record ever accorded Blücher and the Prussians the credit they deserve. To explain briefly:

After the defeat at Ligny, the Prussians were chased by Marshal Grouchy with a gross total of 32,000 troops and 96 guns, heading in the direction of Wavre on to which von Bülow's corps was coming in from Liège area. What Blücher ordered on the frightful night of 17th/18th June was that the defeated units from Ligny and any forces from the Prussian 1st, 2nd and 3rd Corps should stand and fight *south of Wavre*, so that von Bülow's force, coming from the east could move straight through Wavre, unimpeded, and go on westwards to join Wellington. This, without question, meant at least exposing and possibly sacrificing half the Prussian army to the onslaught of Marshal Grouchy. Blücher is said to have declared that 'It is not at Wavre but at Waterloo that the campaign is to be decided.' Though a fine sentiment, that is a remark to be taken as concocted after the victory, for at the time nobody, certainly not Blücher, knew for sure where the show-down would take place.

It is an extraordinary fact, and worthy of close attention by participants in a wargame, that even at this late hour Wellington was suspicious of the apparent intentions of Napoleon.

The Duke had in his hands reports of Napoleon moving from Ligny to Quatre Bras. The 'mean line of advance' was W.N.W.

At the same time, Napoleon had deliberately split his army, and the right wing was advancing northwards towards Wavre, direction N.N.W.

Was it Napoleon's plan to continue W.N.W., on through Nivelles, across to Halle . . . and *then* wheel right as the force at Wavre wheeled left, so that Wellington would be trapped in pincers, having to fight east and west at the same time?

Thank heavens, the Duke doubtless exclaimed in more everyday army terms, that the Netherland force of 18,000 under Prince Frederick was on that flank, guarding against any surprise manoeuvre by Napoleon in that quarter.

He need not have worried. Napoleon, frustrated and furious at the enemy's escape from Quatre Bras and Ligny, now eagerly sought a show-down without further delay. In the words of *La Marseillaise: Le Jour de Gloire est arrivé.*

But another message now arrived from Blücher.

Wellington could hardly believe his eyes, but his Prussian co-commander had formally demanded that if Napoleon did not attack on the 18th then the entire Prussian and Allied armies *must* attack Napoleon on the 19th!

Not for nothing had the old Prussian, now in his 73rd year, been nicknamed 'Marshal Vorwärts'.

11
Let Battle Commence

Sunday, 18th June, 1815
At dawn torrents of rain were still descending on the scene of the impending battle. It had rained throughout most of the dark night; and the wretched soldiers, on both sides, had endured the wet misery without protection.

One of the minor mysteries is that nobody of any consequence seems to have caught cold, had a stiff neck, suffered rheumatic pains or contracted pneumonia in the soaking conditions. It must have been with relief that the bugles summoning to form up were heard because at least the action of movement would stimulate the circulation in cramped and damp limbs.

However, the rain began to lessen and then stop. The fields were sodden, but the cyclonic depression had moved on so that there was no more rain that day. From 8 a.m. (08.00) onwards the weather improved, and 12 hours later there was a clear sky and moonlight night to follow.

It is now necessary to bear in mind that the French

were occupied with two thrusts northwards, in parallel. As the divisions of Napoleon's force moved into battle array with the motion of a surrealistic pavane, some 10 miles to the east the army of Marshal Grouchy was advancing towards Wavre.

Napoleon had to wait until far into the late forenoon for Ney's full force to come up from the south. He had expected Ney to appear pronto – in fact Ney was delayed by the state of the roads and countryside.

Once again, Wellington was still half-convinced that Napoleon would swing right across his front; and so, in a manner that now seems incredible, he maintained the 18,000 troops to his far distant right, athwart the Mons road – and they took no part in the critical action of the main battle. Grouchy must bear criticism for remaining out on the French far right wing, so also must Wellington stand in error for leaving Prince Frederick to do nothing on the British right.

Both commanders, and of course their troops, were in sight of each other. Considering the scale of the conflict and the tens of thousands involved at any one moment, the arena is astonishingly small. The extended maximum 'width' of the battle front was no more than 4 miles (6 km.), from Braine l'Alleud in the west to Paris Wood in the east, and just over $2\frac{1}{4}$ miles (3.5 km.) from Mont Saint Jean ridge in the north to Rossomme in the south. In fact, Braine l'Alleud (the name means 'The Freeholding of Braine') was not involved in the fighting which did not cross the Nivelles road. The actual main struggle was confined to some 1,200 yards (1,100 m.). As a reminder, and subject to the detailed analysis of the statistics as set out on p. 65, the comparative totals were

Wellington 49,608 infantry 12,402 cavalry 5,645 artillery
                                                                                                      156 guns
Napoleon   48,950 infantry 15,765 cavalry 7,232 artillery
                                                                                                      246 guns

The disposition of the forces on each side appears in detail on Fig. 6 opposite, which should be studied with

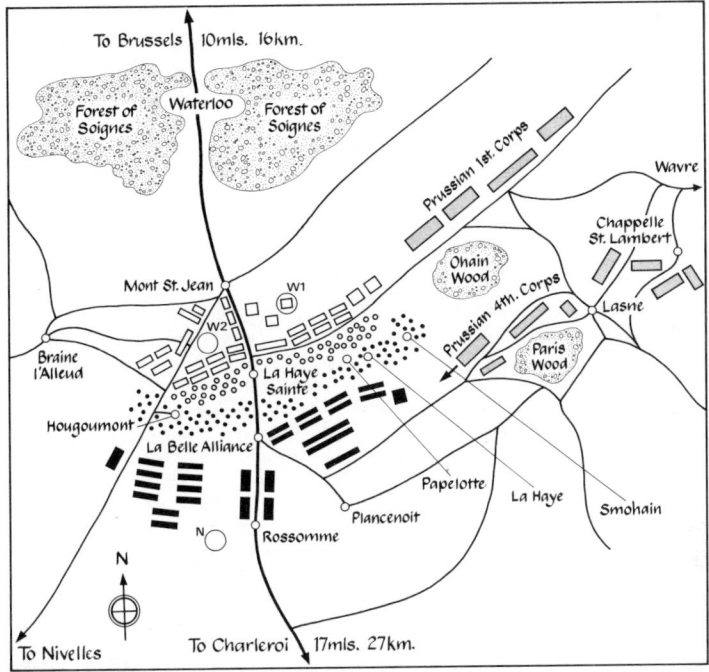

Fig. 6. General dispositions of the Allied, Prussian and French armies during the battle. Note that this diagram can only give a static representation of a very fluid action. It cannot therefore be claimed as accurate for any specific time during the battle. The sequence of events was as follows:
1. The British and allied force took up position late on 17th June.
2. The French formed up early on 18th June.
3. The battle began with an attack on Hougoumont at 11.35.
4. The battle then switched to the French right for a short period.
5. Major attacks were then launched, first by the French left, and then by the French right.
6. The first Prussian troops appeared in the late afternoon, by Paris Wood.
7. The French moved forces against the Prussians at Plancenoit.
8. At the same time the French attacked against the English left.
9. The Prussians began to come in from Ohain Wood.
10. The Imperial Guard attacked on the French left, in two successive columns.
11. The Guard attack broke, its men scattering toward French right.
12. The French right began to collapse.
13. The British charged the French left.
14. French army broke and fled in disorder, pursued by the Prussians.

Figs. 4 and 5 (pages 88 and 92). The latter depict the situation as seen by the respective commanders looking one south and the other north.

The battle began at the order of Napoleon who at 11 a.m. (11.00 hours) ordered a frontal attack. This was against the advice of his subordinates Soult and Reille, both of whom had suggested an encircling manoeuvre as opposed to a head-on clash.

The engagement began with the artillery of the 2nd Corps (Reille) opening fire on the so-called château farm-house of Hougoumont. This attack was intended as a diversion, and the French leader (Jerome) was at fault in not understanding this.

Hougoumont was to prove a persistent point of festering aggravation to the French. It must be assumed that Napoleon ordered it to be attacked because he thought it would soon be overwhelmed.

So its capture was ordered as a sort of late-morning exercise, whilst more troops came up from the south. But in the event it was attacked from 11.30 to 13.00 without capture and with considerable losses. It was the first of many bungled assaults by the French; and though, for the purposes of continuing the action of the main narrative Hougoumont is not referred to much more, it was continuously in the battle throughout the day.

Doubtless irritated by this pin-prick delay on his extreme left, at 1 p.m. (13.00 hours) Napoleon was about to obliterate with batteries of artillery another sore thumb in the picture he looked over, namely the buildings of La Belle Alliance. However just before he gave the order to open fire a movement of the enemy on his extreme right was pointed out to him. With his spyglass clapped to his eye, Napoleon saw emerging from Paris Wood troops which could only be Prussian.

In fact, these troops were the vanguard of von Bülow's 4th Corps, coming in from the village of Chapelle Saint Lambert, 6 miles (10 km.) to the N.E.

Realising the possible danger on his right, and aware that an engagement there would upset his main plan for a frontal attack, at 1 p.m. (13.00 hours) he despatched a most urgent message to Marshal Grouchy to join him at once on his extreme right and there deal with a small Prussian force.

This message from Napoleon did not reach Grouchy until 5 p.m. (17.00 hours).

Here we break away from the main action, which of course has not yet developed, to spotlight Grouchy who, in accordance with Napoleon's orders, had set off from Ligny in pursuit of the Prussians. Because of the weather, he too made a late start in the forenoon of Sunday, 18th June; and he had pressed northwards in good order ever ready to stop and fight if the retreating enemy would stand their ground.

Consequently, though Grouchy's very considerable force had begun to move at about 08.00 hours he was barely half-way to Wavre at 11.35 when the sound of gunfire was borne on the wind coming from the west. This, of course, was the opening bombardment at Hougoumont.

At once, General Gérard (commanding the Army of the Moselle, the French 4th Corps) urged that the pursuit of the Prussians should be abandoned, and that Grouchy's army should wheel left towards the sound of the battle.

Grouchy was now on the horns of a dilemma: if he disobeyed Napoleon's instructions by acceding to Gérard's proposal then certainly the Prussians would escape and his presence at the action vaguely somewhere in the west could well be superfluous. On balance, he decided to stick to the orders and the agreed plan . . . and was quite unaware that only $1\frac{1}{2}$ hours later Napoleon would issue orders exactly on the lines of Gérard's suggestion.

When that instruction from Napoleon finally reached Grouchy four hours after dispatch – it was far too late because if Grouchy had then at once broken off the engagement with the Prussians that he was conducting in a disjointed fight just short of Wavre he would still not have had time to move his army westwards cross-country to reach Napoleon before nightfall . . . and that would have been far too late.

Grouchy in fact was on a loser all the way. Due to the foresight (and orders) of Blücher, von Bülow's force had moved smartly westwards and had already cleared Wavre by the time Grouchy came up from the south. The forces he engaged by Wavre were not von Bülow's, as had been expected, but those of the 3rd Corps (Thielman, who had retreated north on Blücher's orders).

What must remain baffling is the sorry story of miscommunication in the completely 'dead' area between Napoleon and Grouchy. Admittedly the gap between the two was of open country with no good connecting roads, but, factually, it took four hours for Napoleon's message to reach Grouchy.

With the appalling farce of communication gone mad in the case of Drouet d'Erlon only two days previously, it might be thought that any common-sense commander would have organised visual communication to prevent any repetition of the military snarl-up. But nothing was done; the French failure can be attributed in no small degree to communication bungling.

All the same, this incident must not lead to thinking that had Grouchy wheeled westwards when Gérard wanted him to, the issue would have been all over for Wellington. Indeed, it probably would not have made a tremendous difference – Grouchy would have come upon von Bülow's corps, and there would, possibly, have been a battle way out on the French far right. But *that* would not have affected the overall and ultimate issue of Prussians reinforcing the Allies under Wellington, for reasons which appear immediately below.

Grouchy now disappears from the battle of Waterloo: he has a part to play, later, as the campaign is wound up after Napoleon's defeat, and that will be discussed in good time.

Now to return to the main battlefield, with Napoleon about to assault at La Belle Alliance.

About 1 p.m. (13.00 hours)
The resistance at Hougoumont had proved far more stubborn than expected.

It also involved a loss of face in that the attack was under the command of Prince Jerome, Napoleon's brother.

Column after column of French debouched on this isolated farm, and although the French penetrated the copse (built around the house as a wind-break) they could not dislodge a party of British Guards in the house itself. All the while, of course, round and about Hougoumont fierce clashes flared up time and again, and at one the whole of Byng's brigade was involved in a furious battle with surging waves of Frenchmen who gained a little only to lose it in quick time.

The struggle for Hougoumont spread eastwards like a prairie fire, and soon the engagement became general all along the opposing lines. Thinking he had spotted a weakness (which it was always the job of the swarms of skirmisher *tirailleurs* to create), Napoleon called on Ney to make a thrust on the centre and left-centre of Wellington's army.

Ney rapidly jockeyed into attack position no fewer than 18,000 infantrymen, disposed in four massive columns. In support was the dashing cavalry of Kellermann, and also 74 guns were drawn up on a slight undulation that gave them open fire on Wellington's line at a range of about 700 yards (640 m.).

Ney's orders were to capture La Haye Sainte, continue directly on to take Mont Saint Jean, and then swing across between that village and Waterloo village, thus to cut off retreat . . . . or even escape.

This fearsome force began to move forward just after 1 p.m. (13.00 hours), and because of the undulation of the ground the gunners were able to fire directly at the Allied opposition over the heads of the advancing infantry.

One French column headed for the east side of the Charleroi road; the other three made for the Duke's centre. The point of attack for this minor force was that position occupied by the Dutch and Belgian brigade commanded by Bylandt. Doubtless, Napoleon had spotted where the weakness lay, for as the Frenchmen came up the slope with, as usual in the pattern of this type of attack, the *tirailleurs* fanning around in the fore, so the entire Dutch-Belgian brigade turned and fled in panic, pounded by the French artillery which of course was now concentrated on the weak point in preparation for the infantry break-through. In parallel, of course, the three columns continued their assault on the centre (west of the Charleroi road).

Fortunately, the gap created by the fleeing Dutch and Belgians was immediately filled by the infantry brigades under Pack and Kempt who had taken part in the battle at Quatre Bras. Here the divisional commander was the redoubtable Sir Thomas Picton, the finest type of English general who had energetically set about welding the two depleted English infantry brigades into one force that amounted to about 3,000 men. This force now had to face approximately four times that number as Ney, seeing the break in the English line, turned troops to exploit the advantage.

Clearly confident that the English would flee like the Dutch and Belgians, the French came on in column; and just as the French subordinate commanders gave the order for their columns to deploy – that is to say at the moment of passing confusion as the ranks were changing formation – with a mighty cry Picton yelled to Kempt's brigade to fire a volley and then charge.

At a distance of only 30 yards a terrible hail of bullets scythed down the front ranks of the advancing French, and seconds later – even as Picton himself fell dead, shot through the head as he led the charge – the French were being stuck like pigs by the long bayonets of the fighting demon English.

The French advance checked – and was given the

bayonet. The follow-up ranks saw the fate of their comrades, and reeled back before the bloody bayonets coming on for *them*.

All this desperate scene had been followed closely by the English cavalry, and at the exact moment for maximum effectiveness Ponsonby's brigade thundered forward. This was the heavy cavalry of the Union Brigade, so-called because it comprised English, Scots and Irish. With sabres flashing the cavalry now cut down the disorganised French infantry in hundreds – many of those who had dodged the infantry bayonets were now chopped to pieces by the cavalry. Mad with the success of the charge, the cavalry turned on the 74 guns that had brought such cruel casualties earlier in the battle, and now the artillerymen were sabred, the traces of the guns severed, and the wretched horses used to draw the guns had their throats cut.

Scenting a major victory, the cavalry of Lord Edward Somerset and Sir William Ponsonby plunged on, ignoring the recall sounded by the cavalry commander, the Earl of Uxbridge, who had seen the danger into which his two gallant subordinates were rushing. Suddenly the nature of the combat changed, for it was now Somerset's Life Guards, Dragoon Guards and The Blues versus the cuirassiers of Kellermann's squadrons. This French steel-clad formation had overrun opposition at La Haye Sainte on the Charleroi road; and, in a victorious spirit, it now rode forward to take on the English. At once seeing the challenge, Lord Uxbridge led the Household Brigade into a head-on clash with Kellermann's cuirassiers, and in seconds a furious mounted battle was in progress. The casualties were dreadful, but the attacking English were undaunted. Gradually the French began to give way, and once that had begun, in quick time Kellermann's starred force was in full retreat.

Unsupported, and in danger of being isolated, the Household Brigade was now checked and brought back to re-form with the heavy cavalry of the Union Brigade.

The French thrust on the centre had failed, and the attack on the English left wing had been routed with very heavy losses. On the French far left, Hougoumont had still not been taken, and fighting was continuing there unabated.

On the French far right the small initial force of Prussians had grown considerably. At 2.30 p.m. (14.00 hours) the French were no further forward. There were heavy casualties on both sides, and the only triumph was the death of a very senior English commander (Picton).

The only thing left for Napoleon to do was to make another and bigger assault, and bring off a *coup* before any serious threat developed on the extreme right of the French army.

This is a convenient point to make clear that on the French right there were *two* forces of Prussians coming in to confront the French.

The first Prussian force consisted of troops of von Bülow's 4th Corps which, as stated, had been observed N.E. of Napoleon's command post. These were sighted at Paris Wood.

The second force approached (also from the east) on a parallel road, just to the north. These were troops from Zieten's 1st Corps, coming from Ohain Wood, just north of Paris Wood.

12
The Gamble that Failed
◆◆◆◆◆◆

The tempo of the battle now changed again – and there is a point to note here as regards a wargame, a point not made in any of the numerous reference works. This is that into the historical narrative is written facts which were only revealed *after* the battle was over. This particularly applies to the size of the forces engaged: for it is possible, though improbable, that each commander knew the precise numbers of troops engaged on his own side, but it is absolutely impossible to him to have known the score of the opponent. Indeed, in the case of Napoleon he did not even know where Grouchy was; and, at one point in the sequence that is about to unfold, it is clear that had he known Wellington's position he could have won the battle – probably if not certainly.

For example, Napoleon could be presumed to guess that the Duke would bring in to his aid the 18,000 troops way out west, guarding the Mons road (instead of waiting for help from the Prussians in the east); but he, who was not even in contact with his own forces a bare 10 miles on his right with Grouchy, could not know how threadbare was the English defence line. For, unlike Wellington who could overlook the entire small area of the battle, Napoleon at best could observe only a part because the English held the crest of the ridge and thus kept out of view of those below, and Napoleon in the distance, even though the French had an observation platform erected.

What Napoleon realised at this stage was that time was running out. He knew he had to wipe out the English force to have any chance of victory. Apart from the Prussians, who clearly only remained in the conflict because the English had not given way (as they *ought* to have done, like the Dutch and Belgians who ran), Napoleon knew that the Russian and Austrian armies had mobilised and were marching towards French frontier positions – a fact which probably most of his own staff did not know. Therefore, on a long term basis, what he had to do was to win this present battle with a minimum of loss, conserving his forces (and especially his veteran forces) for battles yet to come. That fact surely explains his braggart report of victory at Ligny – it was addressed to the Parisians but it was intended to re-awaken the fear of Napoleon in his long-standing Russian and Austrian enemies.

Having failed to penetrate and conquer the English left, the French attack was now switched to the centre and left. A furious preliminary cannonade began, but far from subduing opposition it merely drew equivalent 'tit-for-tat' bombardment from the English artillery. The blunt fact was that the English possession of La Haye Saint and Hougoumont prevented Napoleon's gunners from getting near enough for devastating fire; and thus the possession of these two forward points now became the aim of the attacks at, respectively, the French centre and left.

After half-an-hour of cannonade, the French cavalry were therefore brought to bear on the vital positions, and fresh troops were brought up from the considerable reserves Napoleon still had over and beyond the Imperial Guard, which had so far taken no part in the conflict.

And at about 3.30 p.m. (15.30 hours) squadron after squadron of heavy cavalry rode in to attack the English right, by-passing Hougoumont and ascending the muddy slope at the best speed they could make. Such charges by cavalry could not, of course, be withstood by the forward artillerymen who now adopted the tactics described in detail on p. 46. Briefly, they *ran back*, indicating flight and thus encouraging the French cavalry who accordingly were drawn into range of massed volleys from the stationary infantry behind the gun positions. Squadron after squadron saw apparent victory vanish like a soap bubble, for when they were unable to break the infantry squares and were forced to retire back to their start point, so the allied artillerymen would re-appear from the shelter of the squares to resume their cannonade.

In this piecemeal fashion, the strength of the heavy cavalry – the cuirassiers – was whittled away and finally broken.

Let us now return to the start of the attack, and consider the infantry commanded by Drouet d'Erlon (who of course was under Ney). The attacks of the foot soldiers had been made in column, a sort of greatly elongated rectangle. The idea was to present, on advancing, the minimum target to the opposition *ahead*, and for the column to fan out when some 50 yards from the enemy and make a bayonet charge. These tactics had been resoundingly defeated, and had been followed by the rebuff to the cavalry.

Now consider the second stage of the attack, on the English right and on the French left. Here, as shown above, the heavy cavalry had borne the brunt of the attack (as it were, changing places with the infantry attack on the French right).

That is to say, the French had now tried two methods

of attack and the English had broken both. The attacks had failed; the defence had not been broken; but the defence could not attack in riposte because it was clearly visible that Napoleon still had formidable reserves for further attack in the shape of the Imperial Guard.

Hence, what was later called a good slogging match (as in boxing terms) or, in the Duke's own phrase, 'hard pounding', now took place whilst Napoleon (who still held the initiative) considered what to do.

Napoleon had by now dismounted, because of the excruciating pain caused by his anal affliction. He was positioned on a little hillock near La Belle Alliance. A large table had been taken from the kitchen of one of the houses; this furniture was used for his maps. His telescope was at hand. Marshal Soult stood at his left, watching and sometimes brusquely consulted. The rest of the staff were to Napoleon's rear, mounted.

He was at this table position for a long time; in fact for so long that one of Wellington's gunners reported that he had Napoleon in his sights but at extreme range, and was ready to open fire. Instantly the Duke refused permission, exclaiming (according to Captain Siborne) 'No, I'll not allow it. It is not the business of commanders to be firing on each other.'

By about 5 p.m. (17.00 hours) Ney had to face the fact that his vaunted cavalry had failed against the English right. Thus, whilst the cavalry assault was allowed to diminish during the next half-hour, he prepared an infantry attack. The last cavalry attack in this series came about 6 p.m. (18.00 hours), and close on its heels a mass of 6,000 infantry moved forward – to be met by an horizontal hail-storm of bullets fired in scything volleys; at the same time cannon poured shot into the massed targets. Over the piles of dead and dying a significant advance was nevertheless made, La Haye Sainte being captured. The attacking troops moved closer to the English centre where, of course, they now not only received the full blast of the defence in front of them but also cross-fire from the Duke's men on the slightly curving ridge.

However, the pressure was enormous: in a battle of sheer attrition the English must mathematically lose, but fortunately neither Ney and, especially, Napoleon realised how dangerously near the margin Wellington was. The English troops were nearing their limit, not so much in spirit as in supplies of ammunition and reserves to replace the killed or wounded. Bitter fighting still raged at and around Hougoumont, and the French on their right wing had advanced again to re-take the position of Papelotte – uncomfortably close to the English line. Furthermore, until the promised support from Zieten's 1st Corps came in from the east the English had no more reserves to put into the fighting line.

It seems likely that Ney did in fact appreciate something of the Duke's situation, for he despatched a message to Napoleon, who was still at La Belle Alliance, asking for further, comparatively small, infantry support at once.

This request Napoleon refused out of hand for a very good reason, even though he was holding no fewer than 14 battalions of the Guard in reserve. On the French right flank, the force of Prussians which had been sighted hours before (Bülow's 4th Corps) had now swept in, and after fierce fighting had driven back the French. The Prussian force now occupied the site of Plancenoit. To this scene of action Napoleon had already despatched the Young Guard under Duhesme to support Lobau's infantry and Domon's horse, and though this force had stayed the Prussian advance there was now, at about 6.15 p.m. (18.15 hours) a distinct possibility that the Prussians could sweep in and cut across the French rear, forward of Rossomme.

To counter this threat the Emperor despatched two battalions of the Old Guard to wipe out the Prussians at Plancenoit – and in so doing he had to deny Ney the vital extra infantry that might have tipped the balance against the exhausted English. The Old Guard did what they had been sent to do. Plancenoit, and indeed beyond, was cleared of the Prussians, and the threat on the French extreme right removed . . . but while that brisk action by fresh French troops against tired Prussians was taking place there arrived in Wellington's front line the necessary replacements in men and ammunition to restore the threatened defences.

The Gambler's Throw

There was now a critical point in the battle.

With hindsight it would probably have paid Napoleon to order a full-scale withdrawal on Charleroi, thus saving his army to fight again in another place. But political factors now rose superior to military commonsense: at all costs, even at a gamble, Napoleon now had to seek a decisive action leading to a French victory.

So, the decision taken, he abandoned his farm-house table and maps, and at indescribable personal agony mounted his white charger (to make sure his troops identified him quickly and clearly) and rode to display himself before the uncommitted mass of the Imperial Guard.

True, he had now given orders for the infantry replacements for which Ney had asked some time ago, and these had moved off . . . too late to affect the issue because at last the Prussian troops of Zieten's 1st Corps had come down the road from Ohain Wood and had begun to strengthen the entire English left flank.

On that flank the fighting continued with unabated ferocity, and although the action against the English right wing holds most of the drama in that it deals with the Imperial Guard, it is well to remember that the crunch in the end came from the English left wing i.e. it was the French right that first gave way.

Evening, Sunday, 18th June, 1815

Cries of *Vive l'Empereur!* greeted Napoleon as he rode, as at a parade, before the Imperial Guard. The shouts of the soldiers about to be massacred rose even above the constant cannonade which Major Macready of the 30th Foot described as being like a labouring volcano.

It was just after 7 p.m. (19.00 hours) that the Imperial Guard began to move to its preparatory positions, in two columns. When the smoke from the guns permitted, the allied commanders looked down on the fearsome array of splendidly uniformed *fresh* troops of the dreaded Guard.

Ney was placed at the head of 5 battalions of the Middle Guard (about 4,000 men), which were ordered to attack in the space between Hougoumont in the west and La Haye Sainte in the east, in other words against the enemy's right centre. These five battalions advanced individually in columns.

In parallel with Ney, a powerful force commanded by Donzelot was to attack the British centre head-on. And, of course, the French right continued desultory attacks against the Allied left which was continually receiving troops from Zieten's incoming corps.

The French attack opened at the centre, that is with Donzelot's command. Swarms of *tirailleurs* covered the French gunners who were directing devastating fire into the close-packed ranks of their opponents at a range of less than 200 yards (180 m.), for the sheer weight of the attack had placed the artillery ahead of La Haye Sainte. The onslaught fell mostly on the German Legion and the Brunswickers, but though they suffered cruel losses Donzelot was definitely held in check.

Satisfied that this was the case, and observing that every passing minute meant more and more Prussian reinforcements, the Duke now rode across to his right wing.

Ney had started on the left of Donzelot. Instead, however, of leading the Guard straight ahead, that is to say northwards on the line of the Charleroi highway – an advance which would have been complementary to Donzelot's attack – he led the five battalions off to his left, on a line traversing the English front so that instead of being opposite the enemy centre he came up on the English right.

This manoeuvre has never been explained, since militarily it is without any justification. What may have happened is this: Observing the Duke moving from the English left and centre to the right, Ney being somewhat vainglorious though quite unafraid of death might just possibly have had a vision of capturing or killing the Duke in person. What he actually *did* was to expose his men to unprecedented fire, for which action he should have been court-martialled.

Confronting the oncoming Guard were two brigades of English Guards, the nearer to the centre being commanded by Sir Peregrine Maitland, on whose right were the troops of Major-General Sir Frederick Adam.

As the French advanced, so their own gunners had to hold fire lest they shoot down their own troops. This lull in the French cannonade naturally permitted greater freedom of action and movement for the English, who fired disciplined volley upon disciplined volley into the marching and defenceless target of the Imperial Guard which came stolidly on and on. Enemy officers were blown to pieces and their men shattered in ghastly ribbons of flesh and bone, but the superbly drilled Guard moved relentlessly and dumbly on, over the bodies of their dead or maimed comrades.

This horrific scene of pointless attrition did not disturb Ney who, with his own horse shot from beneath him, stood up and with brandished sword led the battered Guard ever onward up the incline. He appeared to have a charmed life, but he certainly was baffled in that though his troops were advancing despite their losses he still could not see the enemy front line.

This amazing fact had a simple explanation. The front rank of the English line was firing prone, from which position the artillery behind them was able to fire over their heads and shattering the enemy at virtually Open Sights range.

Into this trap Ney had led the Guard; and as realisation of their hopeless position penetrated the stunned brains of the French élite the column wavered, hesitated, and gave the opportunity for a bayonet charge by their opponents. The record indicates that the Duke, seeing this split-second point of indecision by the Imperial Guard, shouted to the prone soldiers: 'Up, Guards, and at them!' The words have been disputed, the sentiment cannot be refuted; and, in any case, *si non e vero e ben trovato*, so why crab a good story?

In an instant, as the British bayonets came on, so the French fanned out into a running rabble, downhill, chased by Maitland's men until their sharp recall – for the second column of the Guard was still in being.

However, though disaster had attended the advance of Ney's first column, the second was committed to advance in almost exactly the same pattern and formation, this time from a start point just east of Hougoumont.

The configuration of the ground, imperceptible on even a large-scale map, was such that the oncoming column did not advance directly north but took a line a little to the right, so that it headed for almost exactly the same spot where the first column's advance had been turned to a rout.

The stupidity of this approach is almost unbelievable, because in effect what it meant was that the entire left side of the advancing column was exposed to the fire of Adam's brigade. It was as though the Imperial Guard had deliberately offered itself to be enfiladed, presenting to the enemy the chance of a lifetime. It thus had the full fury of all the fire from Maitland, augmented by the cross-fire from Adam.

No soldiers, however veteran, could prevail against such a defence, for cannon balls and bullets take no account of gallantry and bravery.

Inevitably the Imperial Guard of the second column checked, then halted, and then simply turned and ran downhill in wild disorder in a mad scramble to escape the curtain of fire from their enemy. Worse still, they ran towards their own battalions on the French right –

that is, by La Haye Sainte where a fierce attack was still in progress.

The cry reached the ears of those right flank attackers: *La Garde recule!* And that is as good a euphemism as could be found anywhere because the Imperial Guard had not so much drawn back as been sent in disordered flight. In fact, Napoleon, sizing up the true state of the action, rallied the depleted Guard and at once ordered forward the three battalions of the Old Guard he still had in reserve.

Too late! Wellington had also immediately appreciated that French collapse was imminent. It was now 8.10 p.m. (20.10 hours), some 15 minutes after the second column had fled before Maitland and Adam. He knew that the Prussians under Zieten had now arrived in full force on his left wing so that that flank was without need for further cover by the English.

And the order was given for General Advance on All Fronts!

The Hussars of Vivian's light cavalry were now pitched into the fleeing enemy who had collapsed on the English left (and the French right, under Donzelot). The hussars waded in mercilessly, and the entire French right wing crumbled, moving back in complete disarray on to La Belle Alliance.

After more than nine hours of furious fighting the sun at last shone on Wellington's army – in more senses than one because the clouds had dispersed and the red gold of the last rays of daylight glinted on the bloody blades of avenging lances, swords and bayonets. Desperately, the Guard fell back from Plancenoit, rallying with the remnants of their comrades who vainly re-formed in improvised squares and pockets of resistance; but the Allied tide swept onwards unchecked, giving no quarter to those who for almost a generation had been the scourge of Europe.

Napoleon himself became the centre of one of these Old Guard squares. With him was the ever-faithful Marshal Soult, accompanied by Generals Drouet d'Erlon, Bertrand, Corbineau, de Flahaut and Gourgaud. In defeat and in despair, Napoleon spoke of dying himself on the battlefield; but his entourage in effect bodily removed him from the dreadful scenes, forcing a way through the mass of beaten refugees and just ahead of the pursuing Prussians (who managed to seize his coach). *Le jour de gloire* had indeed arrived – but not for Napoleon.

One of the most pathetic documents of the whole campaign is the despatch Napoleon had sent from the battlefield at 3 p.m. (15.00 hours) with the news for Paris that his victory was no longer in doubt! Six hours later he did not even have an army.

13
At the End of the Day
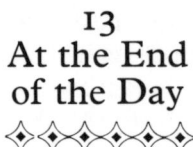

No one general, on either side, figured in all the battles grouped under the umbrella name 'Waterloo', and it seems only fair, therefore, to record the closing scenes through Prussian eyes. The eyes are those of Blücher's Chief of Staff, Lt.-General Count von Gneisenau, who actually concluded his report with the following words:

> In commemoration of the alliance which now subsists between the English and Prussian nations, of the two armies, and their reciprocal confidence, the Field Marshal [Blücher] desired that this battle should bear the name of La Belle Alliance.

No comment was made by the Duke; nor is any needed here . . . except that if, in a wargame, a major variation of the actuality is attempted, then Gneisenau's suggestion might make a suitable substitute for Waterloo, which was so named simply because (a) Wellington had his H.Q. at Waterloo village, and (b) he wrote his victory despatch from that H.Q.

In overall theme and content, the Gneisenau report

supports everything so far set down. In particular he underlines the percipience of Blücher in his (Blücher's) comment that what happened at Wavre was not of decisive consequence and that the issue would be resolved in the conflict at Mont Saint Jean.

The narrative then details how the whole of the Prussian 4th Corps (i.e. von Bülow) and part of the 2nd Corps (i.e. Pirch) had successively come into action, and that the French were fighting with desperate fury. Then:

> At this moment, the first columns of the corps of General Zieten arrived on the points of attack near the village of Smonhen, and instantly charged. This moment decided the defeat of the enemy. His right wing was broken in three places; he abandoned his positions.

The correct name of the village is Smohain. Gneisenau goes on to describe in vivid words what happened after Plancenoit was captured, and the rout of the whole army began:

> ... the retreat became a rout, which soon spread through the whole of the French army, and, in its dreadful confusion, hurrying away everything that attempted to stop it, soon assumed the appearance of the flight of an army of barbarians.
>
> It was half-past nine. The Field Marshal assembled all the superior officers, and gave orders to send the last horse and the last man in pursuit of the enemy. The van of the army accelerated its march. The French being pursued without intermission were absolutely disorganised. The causeway presented the appearance of an immense shipwreck: it was covered with an innumerable quantity of cannon, caissons, carriages, baggage, arms, and wrecks of every kind.
>
> Those of the enemy who had attempted repose for a time were driven from more than nine bivouacs. In some villages they attempted to maintain themselves; but as soon as they heard the beating of our drums

they either fled or threw themselves into the houses where they were cut down or made prisoners. It was moonlight, which greatly favoured the pursuit, for the whole march was a continual chase, either in the cornfields or the houses.

At Genappe, the enemy had entrenched himself with cannon and overturned carriages: at our approach we suddenly heard a great noise in the town, and a motion of carriages. . . .

This must have been Napoleon being whisked away by his escort of Generals, as described already. Other accounts describe how the outriders jostled the wretched refugees to clear the way for the Emperor's coach.

. . . At the entrance to the town we were exposed to a brisk fire of musketry; we replied by some cannon shot, followed by a *hurrah*, and in an instant later the town was ours. It was here that, among the many other equipages, the carriage of Napoleon was taken; he had just left it to mount on horseback, and, in his hurry, had forgotten his sword and hat. Thus the affairs continued till break of day. About 40,000 men, in the most complete disorder, the remains of the whole army, have saved themselves, retreating through Charleroi, partly without arms, and carrying with them only 27 pieces of their numerous artillery.

The report goes on to say that the flight continued beyond the frontier, and assesses that whilst the enemy losses are impossible to total, at least two-thirds of the French army was killed, wounded or taken prisoner. The prisoners included Generals Monton, Duhesme and Compans (a name which does not appear elsewhere and may possibly be a mistake).

After some high-flown comments about the glorious victory, Gneisenau continues:

In the middle of the position occupied by the French . . . is a farm called *La Belle Alliance*. The march of all the Prussian columns was directed towards this farm, which was visible from every side. It was there that Napoleon was during the battle; it was thence that he gave his orders, that he flattered himself with hopes of victory; and it was there that his ruin was decided. There too it was by a happy chance that Field Marshal Blücher and Lord Wellington met in the dark, and mutually saluted each other as victors.

In fact, Napoleon escaped southwards to Philippeville, from which town his army had started a week before with such *panache*. Taking a few hours of rest there, he then issued orders to all French army commanders at their posts elsewhere throughout France to converge on Paris. Marshal Soult was ordered to gather in the tattered remnants of the defeated army and consolidate at Laon, 60 miles (100 km.) to the S.W., whilst Napoleon sped on to Paris before the news of his disastrous defeat became widely known there.

In the wings of this stupendous drama was Marshal Grouchy, still obedient to Napoleon's original orders and in contact with the enemy at Wavre. It seems likely that the possibility of the defeat of his master had not entered into his calculations. At any rate it was not until the early hours of Monday, 19th June, that Grouchy learned of the staggering and unprecedented defeat just a few miles westward of his positions before Wavre.

Once the fact had sunk in, Grouchy reacted with impressive military skill, for his force was now completely outnumbered and isolated behind the troops of the victorious Allies. Skilfully avoiding the highway which he must have guessed, accurately, to be clogged with stragglers and the débris of defeat, he led his divisions southwards to pass on the east side of Namur. Crossing the R. Meuse he kept to the right bank of that river until about the latitude of Givet (on the modern N.51) some 10 miles (160 km.) south of Dinant and well clear of the routed army. He then marched westwards unimpeded, but without military significance, because

Napoleon arrived in Paris in the early morning of 21st June, and abdicated the next day.

To re-track to Wellington who had brilliantly seized the correct moment to order the General Advance. He remained with the foremost troops in pursuit of the fleeing enemy until he reached the area of Rossomme at which he arrived as the moon was rising. Satisfying himself that the rout was effective, and that the French had not been rallied to resume battle, he turned back along the Charleroi road towards La Belle Alliance where at 9.15 p.m. (21.15 hours) he met Blücher. There, as described by Gneisenau, each commander greeted the other as victor. Such compliments having been exchanged it was immediately agreed that the English army had had its measure of fighting for that day and was now exhausted, so that the pursuit of the fleeing French should be undertaken mainly by the Prussians.

Wellington's Dispatch

It will be recalled that on Thursday, 15th June, the Duke of Wellington had, with deliberate calculation, attended the Ball given in Brussels by the Duchess of Richmond; and that he was still at that festive occasion at 3 a.m. (03.00 hours) on Friday, 16th June. All through Saturday and Sunday he had been in command of, effectively, at least two major battles – at Quatre Bras and then Waterloo – and in the early hours of the Sunday night, with the French in flight, he had been a-horse as far as the village of Rossomme, 4 miles south of Waterloo village.

He was 46 years of age (he was to live to be 83!); yet despite the fatigue imposed by the fury of the past four days, on Monday, 19th June, Wellington made a dispatch of some 2,500 words in impeccable English and in the best prose traditions of Caesar's *Gallic Wars*. It was formally addressed to the Minister for War in the Tory administration of the Earl of Liverpool, with King

George III in his dotage and the fabulous Prince of Wales ('Prinny') as Regent.

The text of Wellington's message was published in a special edition of *The London Gazette*, and it subsequently appeared in almost every newspaper in the land. It is worth noting the date-lines; the example quoted below is taken from the *Sussex Weekly Advertiser*, or *Lewes and Brightelmston Journal*.

GLORIOUS VICTORY

Wellington and Old England

FOR EVER!

Huzza! Huzza! Huzza!

The London Gazette Extraordinary
of Thursday, June 22, 1815

Downing-Street, June 22, 1815.
Major the Hon. H. Percy arrived late last night with a dispatch from Field Marshal the Duke of Wellington, K.G., to Earl Bathurst, his Majesty's Principal Secretary of State for the War Department, of which the following is a copy:

Waterloo, June 19, 1815.
My Lord – Bonaparte having collected the 1st, 2d, 3d, 4th and 6th corps of the French Army and the Imperial Guards, and nearly all the cavalry, on the Sambre, and between that river and the Meuse, between the 10th and 14th of the month, advanced on the 15th, and attacked the Prussian posts at Thuin and Lobez, on the Sambre, at daylight, in the morning.

I did not hear of these events until the evening of the 15th, and I immediately ordered the troops to prepare to march; and afterwards to march to their left, as soon as I had intelligence from other quarters to prove that the enemy's movement upon Charleroi was the real attack.

And so in this terse style the Duke described the course of the actions, and at the 20th paragraph he says:

> I propose to move this morning upon Nivelles, and not to discontinue my operations.
>
> Your lordship will observe, that such a desperate action could not be fought, and such advantages could not be gained, without great loss; and I am sorry to add, that ours has been immense. In Lieutenant-General Sir Thomas Picton, His Majesty has sustained the loss of an officer who has frequently distinguished himself in service and he fell, gloriously, leading his division to a charge with bayonets, by which one of the most serious attacks made by the enemy on our position was defeated. The Earl of Uxbridge, after having successfully got through this arduous day, receiving a wound by almost the last shot fired, which will, I am afraid, deprive his Majesty for some time of his services.

In fact, Lord Uxbridge figures in a remarkable exchange of words invariably quoted in the *obiter dicta* of Wellington, thus:

Uxbridge: I have lost my leg, by God!
Wellington: By God, and have you!
(from the *Oxford Dictionary of Quotations*).

Giving generous mention to all who figured prominently in the battle the final three paragraphs run:

> The operation of General Bülow, upon the enemy's flank was a most decisive one; and even if I had not found myself in a situation to make the attack, which produced the final assault, it would have forced the enemy to retire, if his attacks should have failed, and would have prevented him from taking advantage of them, if they should unfortunately have succeeded.

I send, with this dispatch, two eagles, taken by the troops in this action, which Major Percy will have the honour of laying at the feet of his Royal Highness.

I beg leave to recommend him to your Lordship's protection. I have the honour, &c
                                                    WELLINGTON

With the despatch was included a list of 36 officers killed and 80 wounded (many cited as dangerously or severely). The killed were headed by His Serene Highness the Duke of Brunswick, Lieutenant-General Sir Thomas Picton, Major-General Sir W. Ponsonby, followed by four full Colonels and five Lt.-Colonels. The wounded included General his Royal Highness the Prince of Orange, Lieutenant-General the Earl of Uxbridge, Lieutenant-General Sir Charles Alten, Major-Generals Cork, Barnes, Kempt, Halkitt, followed by five Colonels and seventeen Lt.-Colonels.

On the overall battle the Duke of Wellington made a positive comment the exact wording of which is variously cited: it is, of course, possible that Wellington expressed the same notion in different words at different times to different people:

'There is nothing so dreadful as a great victory – except a great defeat.'

'Nothing except a battle lost can be half so melancholy as a battle won.'

'The next greatest misfortune to losing a battle is to gain such a victory as this.'

Information as to casualties is scrappy and generally unreliable; but Haydn's famous reference book gives the following: 'Of the British (23,991) 93 officers and 1,916 men were killed and missing, and 363 officers and 4,560 men wounded – total 6,932; and the total loss of the allied army amounted to 4,206 killed, with 14,539 wounded and 4,321 missing, to make a total of 22,976 *hors de combat*.' Those figures are for Waterloo as such, and to them should be added, with discretion, figures cited in the journal of a surgeon with the army for the engagement at Quatre Bras on 16th June: 2,300 British killed, plus 2,500 other allied troops killed. The *Encyclopaedia Britannica* states that Wellington lost 15,000 dead and wounded; the Prussians 7,000; the French approximate 25,000 with 8,000 prisoners and 220 guns.

Whatever the true figures, the French army was broken and the Allied Armies sufficiently intact to restore peace to a Europe sick to death of war.

14
Assessing the Battle
◆◆◆

With the course and result of the battle known, we can now assess the success, or otherwise, of the tactics used at any particular stage in the conflict.

Tactics can be defined as the manner and method of disposing military forces in battle; and the clear lesson to be learned from Waterloo is that infantry of good calibre, with the right arms, discipline and training, could beat the far more glamorous cavalry.

The amazing thing is that Napoleon, who had created the Imperial Guard, had apparently not learned this lesson despite his earlier widespread victories. But then in no previous campaign had he come up against an honest-to-God infantry commander (except possibly at Borodino where the result of the battle was indecisive).

On the other hand, Wellington was basically an infantryman, his own Regiment being the 33rd Foot.

It could be said that whereas Napoleon had had (in terms of the theatre, for he was a most dramatic commander) repeat performances of the same play with different casts all over Europe, the vast experience of

Wellington embraced many different plays in India and Spain, with many different casts.

In the cold light of hindsight it is difficult to account for Ney's desperate assault in the early afternoon of 18th June.

It must show as a basic misconception of the situation that Napoleon ordered an attack uphill on a muddy ground against a position manned by infantry disposed under the direction of a most experienced commander such as Wellington.

Secondly, although Napoleon had the men to manoeuvre to surround Wellington long before attempting any such attack, in fact he deliberately chose a head-on frontal clash with his own troops unprotected, uncovered and unsupported.

Thirdly, he chose Ney to command the critical make-or-break onslaught. Ney, however, was obviously 'battle-drunk' after his failure at Quatre Bras. The best thing that could have happened to Ney was that he should have been killed when leading his men against the impossible odds of the English defence.

Fourthly, it is quite inexplicable that Napoleon should have let Grouchy remain out on the far right wing, and equally beyond comprehension that Grouchy did not have a communication link with Napoleon. The only possible answer to this conundrum is that, at about 3 p.m. (15.00 hours) when Napoleon despatched a message to Paris to say that victory was imminent, at that time the Emperor must really have believed he was going to smash the opposition. Hence he would have considered it invaluable to have Grouchy coming in on the right as he moved in to capture Brussels after the battle.

However, what was done was done, so let us consider the appalling facts of Ney's attack (which, of course, Napoleon was in a position to oversee).

To recapitulate, between 1 p.m. and 2 p.m. (13.00–14.00 hours) Ney was in command of 18,000 troops which were formed up in battle array.

The records say that he had three divisions, but it is not clear whether that was three Divisions in a strictly military sense or whether the 18,000 troops had been divided into three loosely organised formations for the purpose of the attack.

There is no dispute, however, that each formation was in column form, and that the total came to one-quarter of all the troops under Ney's command.

Furthermore, each column was 200 men abreast, with between 24 and 27 ranks in depth.

Let us analyse this positive statement. There seems no way of knowing what was the allotted width occupied by one soldier, but what is known is that in the Royal Navy, where in the matter of slinging hammocks there was a parallel case with that of a soldier standing in line, the space allowance per man on each mess deck was 27 inches.

Using that yardstick, which must give an *absolute minimum* answer when considering infantrymen in their battle equipment, each column was 200 × 27 inches wide i.e. 150 yards wide (say 140 m.).

Similarly, for marching troops, the space occupied on average by one man (from the heel of the left foot of the man in front to the heel of the left foot of the man behind him) is generally accounted as 38 inches (though in some special parade formations it can be much less, and on a route march it can be a little more). Using, for convenience, 36 inches, then with an average of 25 such ranks the length from the front to the rear would be 175 ft. (160 m.).

What has to be appreciated is that within this compact area, which is roughly equivalent to only $1\frac{1}{2}$ football (soccer) pitches, there were 200 × 25 (= 5,000) soldiers marching into a heavy concentration of cannon and musket fire.

There were three such columns of standing/marching targets into which the full fury of the defensive fire could be directed without little chance of missing.

That Napoleon, or Ney, or Drouet, or any of the

subordinate commanders, could accept such conditions for an attack *on the level* and in the dry, would be thought by any normal layman to be military madness – but to have three such columns marching uphill in slippery mud is beyond rational explanation.

Even if it is accepted that such a phalanx would have to bear unprecedented losses, it must be clear that most of the 5,000 men in it would be unable to fire at the enemy because of obstruction by their comrades in arms. Furthermore, to believe that sheer numbers could get to within 50 yards is just possible, but then to expect an uphill charge in the face of point-blank fire – that is not so much military ineptitude as battle insanity.

Napoleon had sneeringly referred to Wellington as a 'Sepoy General'. Had he known his Indian history better he might have been less contemptuous – for it was at Plassey almost exactly 58 years earlier that another English 'Sepoy General' (Clive), with 1,000 British soldiers and 2,000 sepoys, defeated 68,000 Hindus under Surajah Dowlah! And Wellington's record was in no way inferior to Clive's.

Other questions also come to mind when considering the events of that bitterly fought and often confused day – questions that in the past appear to have been not so much unanswered as not even asked.

The first is based on the sustained apprehension by Wellington throughout the preliminaries and (so the evidence would indicate) even right up to the afternoon of the great battle – the fear that Napoleon was really pulling a bluff and that the *real* advance would come on the Mons road.

The mystery is why Napoleon did not in fact take that road. By choosing, when he had unrestricted choice, to move N.E. on to Charleroi the geographical fact is that Napoleon was actually facilitating the union of the Allied army with the Prussians – whereas, had he come via Mons, as Wellington expected, that would have added so much the more distance before Blücher could possibly link with the Duke.

No reference work has explained why Napoleon did not come from Mons. It would, therefore, make an extremely interesting wargame subject to explore the possibilities of the initial concentration of the *Armée du Nord* with a Mons–Brussels approach.

Linked with the above, is the retention by Wellington of some 18,000 troops at Halle – troops which could have been invaluable at two or three critical periods. What was the purpose of 18,000 troops on the Mons road? Such a force would be too small to stop the French main force, and yet was far too big for any localised reconnaissance and covering force.

Again, no satisfactory explanation was put forward by the writers in the years just following Waterloo. However, study of the map may indicate the answer: that Wellington was more than half prepared to have to accept not defeat but wholesale withdrawal at Waterloo; and the line of such a withdrawal would not be back on to Brussels but westwards to Halle – thus drawing Napoleon away from the capital which was of major political significance to French aims.

Of course, there may well have been intelligence records that Wellington destroyed as being useless and irrelevant at the time of victory, and hence completely unknown to either amateur or professional historians. Note, however, the fact that although Wellington's worrying about the possible Mons approach is repeatedly mentioned, there is a singular lack of information about the position, strength, and operational plans of the Russian and Austrian armies that were pledged to fight against Napoleon – and fight till he was overcome.

The more the picture is studied, the more it seems apparent that only a superficial account has been offered by historians of the full facts of the case. For such an expert in manoeuvre as Wellington, with a dozen major victories to his credit in the Peninsular War, it would have to be second nature to have had an escape line planned. The question is whether that also included provision of a fresh, un-battled, force of 18,000 men at Halle? And, of course, one can ask what would have been the result had he brought them into action at (say) the lynch-pin of the battle, Hougoumont farm.

Not surprisingly, Waterloo as a landscape + battle-scene subject has often caught the imagination of painters. Alas, no masterpieces have emerged! Of course, a certain degree of artistic licence is permitted but most of the pictures indicate weather conditions that certainly did not prevail at Waterloo on 18th June, 1815. The wargamer may, however, learn from these artists the enormous difficulty involved in compressing into the confines of even an extra large canvas, a scene from a battle involving not less than 100,000 men.

For the reader able to spend some time in London, the Army Museum is worth a visit, though strangely enough it contains very little specifically connected with Waterloo: just a tattered French standard, an eagle, some swords, and a token selection of uniforms. The Army Museum is in Chelsea, housed in a new building immediately west of The Royal Hospital (the home of the Chelsea Pensioners, founded in 1682 by Charles II). The Royal Hospital, whose small and little-known museum is also well worth a visit, has a Wellington Room, where the Duke's coffin lay before his funeral cortège proceeded to St. Paul's Cathedral for burial. This room contains a huge panoramic picture of the battle in the best mid-19th Century tradition.

In London, of course, one should not miss the Wellington Collection in Apsley House, Piccadilly. Apsley House was the Duke's London residence, and has been preserved as a memorial. The most famous painting there is entitled *The Battle of Waterloo* by Sir William Allan (1782–1850) who was an expert on Russian landscapes and who is tactfully described in the *Dictionary of National Biography* as 'limner to the Queen in Scotland, 1841'. This painting is interesting for several reasons apart from the artistic. First, it shows the battle-scene from the French side, with Napoleon clearly depicted with his staff. Secondly, it shows what the Apsley House official guide describes as 'the town of La Haye Sainte' – there was no town, and not even a village, just a few houses. Thirdly, someone must have briefed the artist on Congreve rockets, because in the picture by the side of the Duke are the 'long flashes' of Congreve rockets which were certainly not in action at 7.30 p.m. (19.30 hours). But perhaps its highest recommendation as a painting was made by the Duke himself, for on first seeing the picture he exclaimed 'Good – very good – not too much smoke'.

The unfortunate fact is that there was no Goya (as in the Peninsular War) to give pictorial realism to this fantastic event. No participant could have looked as spick-and-span as paintings indicate in the best chocolate-box style. As the narrative shows, from Ligny onwards until 08.00 hours on the morning of Waterloo, there had been shocking bad weather, and men and animals had spent the eve of the battle without cover in a downfall of rain. Mud-bespattered uniforms would be everywhere – mud from underfoot, mud kicked up by horses' hooves, mud scattered by cannon shot.

Earlier, mention was made of the great model made by Captain Siborne in the years 1830–38. This diorama was housed in the Royal United Services Institution in Whitehall for decades; but when in 1960 the Army decided to erect its own museum in Chelsea (see above) the intention was to re-house Captain Siborne's mammoth work there. Either from old age or the hazards of removal, the model became damaged, and was quietly removed to Aldershot. It is now said to be in a sadly dilapidated state, beyond repair.

Another interesting point for students of the battle is how vital orders were actually conveyed during the battle (a) on account of the noise from guns and firearms, and (b) over distances beyond the range of even the most powerful human voice. Orders originated from the Duke and his commanders as written messages but there came a point where they had to be transmitted to large numbers of men in the heat of battle. The accepted explanation that bugle calls or drum beats were used for this purpose seems hardly valid on examination. For example, the hearers could literally be deafened by the cannonades, whilst the vital message might suddenly be terminated as the bugler was interrupted in full blast. As a relevant point, the system of orders imparted by bugle calls implies (1) that all situations arising could be covered by a specific sequence of notes; (2) that the bugler should know all the notes for a given order, and (3) that the hearer should accurately interpret the notes he hears. The chances of error must surely have been great, and they would, at Waterloo, have been considerably increased, since Wellington himself complained that he had in the English divisions many raw recruits (who could not possibly have learned quickly the meaning of all the possible bugle calls).

A small clue to the communication problem is to be found in the Muniment Room at Apsley House. Among the glittering displays of batons, orders, plate, swords, banners, telescopes, and personal relics are a few slips of prepared skin bearing the actual pencilled orders by the Duke to unit commanders at Waterloo. Consider what this method meant:
On horseback, the Duke would write a message on a 3" × 4" slip of skin.
This slip would be handed to an officer of the staff to take to the appropriate commander.
The chances for failure in a system of this nature are great; the marvel is that the Duke, or any contemporary Commander-in-Chief, was able to achieve and maintain overall control of the action. It is clear that, as with Nelson and his Captains, the Duke had a highly developed *rapport* with his divisional and brigade commanders who could interpret his thinking in terms of actions. The bugle system must only have applied to

strictly limited local orders such as Advance, Charge to the Right, and so on.

There are also problems arising out of the actions of the French. Nobody has explained why Grouchy, who was essentially a cavalry officer, was sent off with the extreme right wing on an infantry operation. Nor has any reason been given for the delay in summoning Ney from Paris. Nor why, having arrived to take over the left wing, Ney was so completely uninformed of the true position at Quatre Bras when even a recce by one small squadron of the vaunted French cavalry could have made the facts clear.

Then, when Napoleon arrived at Quatre Bras only to find the English had withdrawn and escaped to fight again, what exactly did he mean by his despairing comment: '*On a perdu la France!*' This sentence is translated in some reference books as 'France has been ruined'; but that is an interpretation rather than a translation, and though there could be a finesse of meaning and even a deliberate double meaning with the impersonal '*On a . . .*' the straightforward meaning is 'We have lost France', and the secondary meaning, particular to the circumstances of the absence of French troops at Quatre Bras, is that Ney is responsible for the loss that will arise because of failure to destroy the English. This may be a matter of semantics – but then the whole story of Waterloo is riddled with misunderstandings in communication.

15
Waterloo as a Wargame
◆◇◆◇◆◇◆◇◆

The main action, the confrontation of Wellington and Napoleon, bears the elements of the ancient conundrum of philosophers – what happens when an Irresistible Force meets an Immovable Body? The philosophical answer is that there will be an Unprecedented Event; and that there certainly was at Waterloo.

It therefore follows that no other wargame that aims to simulate history in part has the same degree of speciality as that of Waterloo. In the crudest form, and in the sense of the Duke's own words, there was a prolonged slogging match. At the end of the day the French morale broke under the sustained defence of the British and Allies. The slaughter in numbers of men and animals was immense; and it is difficult to understand, at this distance of time, how some of the detailed actions were able to occur.

As it would be difficult to represent Waterloo adequately as a single wargame, it follows that the wargamer would have to choose some particular part, such as Picton's charge or the late advance of the great column of the Imperial Guard.

In both these examples, as in other actions, the prevailing factor is that at any one 'scene' there is a doubly complex action taking place.

Thus, the cavalry may charge the infantry, but on both sides there is simultaneous artillery.

Hence, what has to be synchronised is that a volley fired almost certainly would coincide with gunfire.

Furthermore, it is not satisfactorily realistic to accord the French the normal advantages for being the attackers. There must be a local rule giving Wellington's forces credit for standing firm after repeated attack by an enemy who normally bore all before him by means of a wave of massed infantry.

Under accepted wargame rules, a volley can be made by 5 men; and a regiment of 20 men equates with 4 volleys. (For 15 men, 3 volleys; for 8 men, 2 volleys; for 7 men, one volley.)

Now the fact is that the French advanced towards the British and Allied lines in column of infantry. For wargame purposes such a column is represented by 20 men, disposed as to 4 men abreast and 5 files deep. Disregarding the fact that soldiers advancing as indicated would never normally be expected to fire at all – their movement would make a mockery of aim – nevertheless in extremity perhaps fire might be opened. Obviously, because of obstruction by their comrades, only the front or lead rank of 4 men can fire on the approach directly ahead, whilst on the flank only the 'outsiders' (5 to each flank) can fire on the enemy. In other words, although on the table there may be a regiment of 20 men, in fact only 12 of them at a maximum can open fire (and the likelihood is that effectively only 4 could bring fire to bear).

In standard wargame rules, with a column of advancing infantry under fire, when their casualties gross one third of their total original strength it is necessary to confirm that the column will charge. This is done by throwing a 4 or 5 or 6 with a dice. If a 1 or 2 or 3 is thrown, then the rules provide for the column to be retreated to its start point.

This leads to intricate problems in the scoring because at a certain stage of losses the column in effect changes its rôle, and instead of attacking it is defending. In the same fashion, the defending British infantry having successfully decimated the oncoming column can change its rôle from defence to attack with a charge and mêlée. The rule in such cases is that the attackers receive a bonus of 1 point for each dice thrown.

Furthermore, a great proportion of the overall action concerned the French cavalry attempting to break the British and Allied defence. Here two points arise:

(1) the defending infantry form into squares. Each square is 60 ft. to one side. The colours are in the centre of the square, and the officers are by the colours. The troops are normally in three rows with (a) the front or outermost row kneeling, holding fixed bayonets as a sort of steel hedge or stockade against the cavalry. (b) and (c) standing behind (a), fire volleys over the heads of the front rank (a), and fire alternatively, one row loading and one row firing.

The point to make here is that the cavalry advance from directly ahead only one side of the square can fire at them (in other words the fire-power of the square is one fourth of its manpower).

The general rule for cavalry advancing on a square is that if on the approach there is a loss of one quarter of their numerical strength then a dice must be thrown to see whether they continue or withdraw. For this, a dice of 4 or less means the cavalry attacking must withdraw out of musket range.

However, if a 5 or 6 is thrown, in these circumstances, the cavalry may advance but it must split (divide) with one part going to one side of the square under attack (i.e. at right angles to the front rank) and the other part to the other side, parallel and opposite. Thus, each of the divided parts of the cavalry is subjected to fire from one side of the square as it rides through.

Now, having divided and being on the two flanks of the square, if the cavalry do not lose one quarter of their total strength, then a further dice is thrown to decide whether they charge the square or not. For this, a 5 or 6 is needed to make a charge; otherwise, the cavalry will have ridden through and wheeled back to start point. In this type of action, for the mêlée between infantry and cavalry, the *infantry* take double score because of their cohesion and morale.

Possibly the next special feature for Waterloo is the effect of gunfire; or rather, the missiles fired. Some explosive shells were used (shrapnell dates to 1803) and there was grape shot and case shot – all having a 'browning' effect, as with a sportsman's shot gun. But a considerable percentage of the artillery fire was with solid iron cannon balls. These frequently cut complete lanes through a close-packed and advancing column of infantrymen. It is a small but important point that the French guns were firing uphill but the British and Allied fire was downhill – so that for the latter not only was the range increased if anything but the roll-on of the solid shot was actually assisted by gravity.

To adjust for this, a suggestion is that before gunfire the type of shot used must be nominated.

Now, for all except solid iron, the scatter element can be provided for by a system of range integrated with fire-zone. Thus, for table distance 36″ maximum range down to 18″ there must be a 6 dice for a hit;

for 17″ down to 9″ a 5 or 6 is needed for a hit;
for below 9″ a hit is made by a 4 or 5 or 6;

Then, with the hit established, throw another dice to give the number of men killed by that hit. That applies against infantry: for cavalry the scores must be halved.

(An alternative method is to have a pre-arranged ring of, say, 2″ diameter; and when a hit is scored then all the enemy covered by that ring – placed with the hit as its centre – would be marked as killed.)

But when, before throwing the dice for gunfire, 'solid shot' is nominated, then to adjust for the penetration and run-on the following table would give the compensation factor:

Dice thrown					1st rank	2nd rank	3rd rank
6 against infantry column kills					3	2	1
5	,,	,,	,,	,,	3	1	1
4	,,	,,	,,	,,	2	1	1
3	,,	,,	,,	,,	2	1	—
2	,,	,,	,,	,,	1	1	—
1	,,	,,	,,	,,	1	—	—

(Against cavalry the run-on of solid shot does not apply, as the horses not the men would be affected.)

In the actual combat, the number of mêlée actions was beyond reckoning; and in converting actuality to a wargame here, it is necessary to have clear rules that give neither opponent any special advantage. To fight the battle over again it is necessary to accept that the cavalry did not beat the squares, and the artillery did not of itself beat infantry or cavalry, *on both sides*. Therefore, special rules must apply for Waterloo.

Hence, in the commonly accepted rules the number of enemy killed in a mêlée is half the score of the dice thrown. A leading exponent of wargames, Mr. Donald Featherstone in his excellent book *Battles with Model Soldiers* published by David & Charles (1970), states that in a straightforward action between two bodies of infantry one dice is thrown for each five men, and the number of enemy casualties is *half* the total score of dice thrown. The same yardstick applies for cavalry versus cavalry. At the same time he gives a bias to the cavalry when in a mêlée with infantry, awarding one point extra for each dice thrown for cavalry.

Nevertheless, in this same book Mr. Featherstone points out that in wargaming, rules are 'gloriously elastic', and that there is no dictate as to what must be done. This is fortunate because with hindsight we know that the Duke's forces suffered total losses of approximately one third and, under some rules, he ought to have retired beaten long before that mark was reached.

Furthermore, in some regards the two forces were divided by the main road running right through the scene of the action (Waterloo to Charleroi); so that there was an action left of that road and, at the same time, a similar action to the right (and necessarily the same for the French).

What we can set down as a guide to making up the components for a wargame is that the Duke lost about 23,000; and that by averaging out the figures the loss on the Duke's left was 1,450 per hour, and on his right the rate was 1,350 per hour. Now, for the opposing forces, the French lost on average 1,200 per hour on their right (i.e. opposing the Duke's left); and 1,550 per hour on their left. All the actions, spread over nine hours, involved infantry and cavalry and artillery, though often the accent was on one more than the other. There is one important fact to remember: it was the boast of the Duke (or at least for the Duke) that he never lost a gun, whereas at Waterloo the French repeatedly lost artillery pieces.

Another aspect of the operation is that necessarily as the long struggle dragged on the numbers on both sides steadily diminished. The figures before the start of the action are available, especially for the French; and they read as follows.

Imperial Guard: 24 battalions, 32 squadrons, 13 batteries, 96 guns.
   Commander: Count Druoet, for Marshal Mortier (sick)
   Old Guard under Friant
   Middle Guard under Morand
   Young Guard under Duhesme

1st Corps was commanded by Drouet d'Erlon 20,564 men 46 guns
2nd Corps   ,,   ,,   Reille   23,161 ,, 46 ,,
3rd Corps   ,,   ,,   Vandamme   15,892 ,, 38 ,,
4th Corps   ,,   ,,   Gerard   14,792 ,, 38 ,,
5th Corps NOT PRESENT IN THIS ACTION
6th Corps was commanded by Lobau   11,192 ,, 38 ,,

Reserve cavalry under Grouchy totalled 12,800 with 48 guns, but did not serve as such under Grouchy opposite Wellington, Grouchy being engaged east of the main action as the narrative relates.

These figures indicate that for a table wargame the reduction factor might well be 1,000 to 1, for the troops and 10 to 1 for the guns.

Another point of special Waterloo import is visibility. In fact, there are two factors bearing on this aspect: the terrain and the smoke of battle.

First, much of the immunity of the British and Allied infantry line was due to their position on the ridge overlooking the shallow valley. This gave them a distinct advantage over any enemy. Conversely, the French attackers had no such cover, and all their manoeuvres were openly visible EXCEPT that, as a second factor, the smoke of battle drifted down into the valley and, at times of cannonade, whole sections of the battle area were obscured.

In that connection, it has to be borne in mind that the heavy rain before the action had ceased; it was June and the heat of the sun would cause a thin ground mist in patches. However this was never as bad as the smoke concentration.

The concentration factor is also especially vital at Waterloo. Apart from the 'side-shows', as a round figure (excluding the baggage trains in the rear of the action on both sides) approximately 120,000 men were massed in an area 3 miles (5 km.) north/south and 4½ miles (7 km.) east/west.

Whatever scale is used, the battle area must be in the proportion of 3 wide to 4½ deep. Clearly, the larger the table space available overall the better for the actions. The Wargames Research Group, in its Rules for the period 1750–1850, cites for scale a ground distance of 1″ representing 10 paces, each pace being 2½ ft., or in metric a scale of 1 mm. = 1 ft. This scale may well be satisfactory for a detailed action, but as simple arithmetic will show it would mean an extra large table to include the whole Waterloo battlefield.

The Wargames Research Group has in fact formulated most comprehensive Rules mainly for Napoleonic actions. In the form of a hand-guide brochure, with a comprehensive score chart, this publication will not only prove a valuable ready-reckoner and scoring aid but will also assist standardisation of points and conditions of play. Copies are obtainable from Mr. B. O'Brien, Secretary, at 75 Ardingly Drive, Goring-by-Sea, Sussex.

Whilst from a wargaming viewpoint the main action of Waterloo presents problems of space and numbers, none of those limitations apply to the preliminary encounters that opened the campaign.

In recapitulation of the narrative, on the evening of Tuesday, 13th June, General Hans Ernst Karl Zieten, commander of the 1st Prussian Corps, was made aware from his reconnaissance troops that the lights of numerous bivouac fires could be seen across the R. Sambre in the vicinity of Beaumont.

There lies an almost perfect set-up for a wargame on established lines, in that the terrain (with river, woods, open fields, etc.) offers full scope for encounter by small, reconnaissance, forces. All the familiar manoeuvres of wargaming can be used here; and it was not until late on 14th June that Blücher ordered Zieten to fall back in an ordered retreat. No *major* action was involved, but there were countless minor brushes. And as no specific details survive in the records of these accounts the wargamer is thus given almost complete freedom of operation using infantry and cavalry in the main.

As has been shown, the main action was a slogging match, but a possibility for an unorthodox approach to a Waterloo wargame exists in the manoeuvres that led up to the final show-down. Nevertheless, none of the main action could have occurred without the preliminary manoeuvres of the armies. Thus if, for a new approach to a wargame, the opposing forces are set out as they were before action began, then the element of chance plus opportunity for individual thinking arises. To give an immediate example: Wellington, fearing that Napoleon would advance along the Mons road to Brussels, kept a large force (approximately 18,000) on his far right wing to cover that possibility. But, for space-movement, and exercising personal decision, the wargamer might well decide to bring in those troops in the west; and, having done so, the threat on the French left would thus surely have cause Napoleon to alter his battlefield dispositions. In general, for this imaginative campaign, a vital factor must be the poor communications of actuality, with simple messages taking hours to pass.

Perhaps the most interesting aspect of this approach to a Waterloo wargame is that in each case the Commander *really* commanded. In actuality, it was Blücher who insisted on going forward to meet Napoleon; and it was Wellington personally who insisted on his line of defence as well as his belief that Napoleon would come on via Mons. Finally, it was Napoleon who required a direct and pitched battle, whereas the consensus of opinion among his subordinates was that a war of manoeuvre would be preferable. Of course, a game played on these lines diverges from the standardised pattern and really does become (in the words of Mr. Donald Featherstone) 'chess with a thousand pieces'.

16
Aftermath

Now in total disgrace amongst the majority of his countrymen, who were angry at the humiliations imposed on them, Napoleon was forced to sign his second, and final, abdication on 22nd June, 1815.

A week later, he departed for Rôchefort (Charente Maritime, Atlantic coast) which he reached on 3rd July with the intention of shipping to America. However the Royal Navy was on watch and blockade, and on 15th July, Napoleon surrendered to Captain Maitland (later Rear-Admiral Sir Frederick Lewis Maitland, (1777–1839), commanding H.M.S. *Bellerophon*. In that warship Napoleon was taken to Torbay (S. Devon) where he was transferred in close custody to H.M.S. *Northumberland* in which, under Admiral Sir George Cockburn (1772–1853), he sailed on 8th August, 1815, for the isolated island of St. Helena in the S. Atlantic. He arrived at his place of exile on 15th October, 1815, and died there on 5th May, 1821. His last words were: 'Tête de l'Armée'.

The allies had entered Paris on 7th July, and Louis

XVIII was restored to the throne, for the second time, on the following day.

The Prussians, whose hatred for the French was unbounded, were restrained by Wellington from sacking Paris. He took a leading part in the peace negotiations where his wise counsel was as much appreciated as his fluency in French. He was appointed Commander of the Army of Occupation, in which post he remained until 15th November, 1818, when the occupation was terminated and the armies disbanded. A month later he re-entered politics: he had been M.P. for Rye (1806); Mitchell (1807); Newport (1807–9); and now he was made Master General of the Ordnance with a seat in the Cabinet (a post he held 1818–27).

The Duke of Wellington had three terms of office as Prime Minister (Tory): January 1828 to June 1830; June to November 1830; and November to December, 1834. He remained in one office or another in politics and the army until 1848, retaining in his old age an active interest in current affairs. He was an almost daily visitor in 1851 to the original Crystal Palace, formally called The Great Exhibition, that stood in Hyde Park a little to the west of his London residence. Already a legend in that he was expected to make oracular pronouncements on almost any subject, his advice was asked by the young Queen Victoria as to what could be done to mitigate the nuisance of sparrow droppings that were ruining her Prince Consort's exhibition. The Duke's laconic answer was: 'Sparrowhawks, Ma'am.'

He died peacefully on 14th September, 1852, aged 83, at Walmer Castle to which he frequently went with pleasure in his capacity of Lord Warden of the Cinque Ports. At his State funeral, far more than a million people lined the route of his cortège from the Horse Guards to St. Paul's Cathedral where he was buried on 18th November.

Memorials and Exhibitions

At or near the battlefield
The house in which Wellington spent part of the night of June 17th–18th, 1815, is preserved, with a museum, in the village of Waterloo.

Opposite stands a church, of which only the round portion (late 17th Century) was in being in 1815. In this church, and its graveyard, are numerous memorials to British officers. In a garden just north of this church is a monument to the amputated leg of the Earl of Uxbridge (Sir Henry William Paget, created Marquis of Anglesey in 1815), commemorating the British cavalry which he led in the battle.

Just south of Waterloo village on the N.5 is the intersection of the Louvain (Leuven)–Nivelles road at the village of Mont Saint Jean. At the Hotel des Colonnes here, Victor Hugo wrote the chapter in 'Les Miserables' about Waterloo. The general British position was to the south of Mont Saint Jean, with the N.5 as its centre meridian. At what is called locally the Waterloo-Gordon cross-roads is the monument to Sir Alexander Gordon (1786–1815), Lt.-Colonel, A.D.C. to Wellington in the Peninsular War and in Belgium, mortally wounded in the battle.

Adjacent is the Monument to the Hanoverian officers, opposite the Gordon memorial; and these two show the true height of the land on this ridge, the shape of which was altered by large-scale removal of earth to make the mound called *La Butte du Lion* or Lion Monument. This dominating artificial hillock (*butte*) was constructed by the Belgians 1823–26 on the spot where the Prince of Orange was wounded; and is surmounted by an iron lion *passant*, headed towards France. *La Butte du Lion* stands 148 ft. high, and its summit is reached by 228 steps. Adjoining this conspicuous landmark is a museum of relics, and a diorama depicting, in particular, a charge led by Marshal Ney.

Further south, ¾ mile away, is the site of *La Belle*

Alliance inn, damaged by fire in 1936 and at one stage centre of the French positions. For long an erroneous inscription stated over the entrance door that this was the meeting place of Blücher and Wellington on the late evening of 18th June (and a famous painting repeats this error). The actual meeting was in fact much further south, near Genappe.

Just east of *La Belle Alliance*, at Plancenoit where the French fought desperately with the Prussians, is a monument to Blücher.

In England

The very name Wellington comes from the manor of Wellington in Somerset (near Taunton), an estate given to the Duke by the nation in 1812.

As the peak of the Duke's military career (say 1810–18) was at a time of great expansion in building (coincident with a population explosion) in London and widely elsewhere in England, countless roads and squares and crescents, etc. were named Wellesley, Wellington, Waterloo, etc. In the current street guide for Greater London there are 70 places named Wellington; 25 named Waterloo; 19 Wellesley; 18 Mornington. Though many of these are not connected directly with the victory of 1815, such buildings as Wellington Barracks in Birdcage Walk, Westminster, and Wellington College, near Sandhurst on the Surrey/Hampshire border, are positively connected with the great soldier.

The Waterloo Chamber in Windsor Castle was created in 1830, and has portraits of the men engaged in the military overthrow of Napoleon.

Abroad

With the defeat at Waterloo a very sore point (still) with the French, there is no place or square or boulevard or rue or avenue in Paris named Waterloo – but Victor Hugo wrote a mournful poem about the battle. There are streets etc. named after Napoleon's successful battles – Wagram, Austerlitz, Marengo, Pyramids, Ulm – but no mention of Waterloo. However, Napoleon has a magnificently solemn tomb in Les Invalides – this is one of the tourist sights of Paris.

In the cemetery at Brussels, a Waterloo Monument was erected in 1890.

The most abiding and interesting memorial to Wellington is his house at Hyde Park Corner. This, popularly known as No. 1 London (because it was the first house on the main route from the west into London) is Apsley House, basically built by Robert Adam for Baron Apsley, later Earl Bathurst, erected 1771–78. In the original it was red brick. It was bought by the Marquis of Wellesley, the Duke's eldest brother, and was sold to the Duke in 1817. In 1829 it had been extensively altered, externally with the Corinthian portico. The real address was 149 Piccadilly, and as such it was conveyed to the nation in 1947.

It is a museum and repository of all manner of Wellingtonia, and has a superb art collection. Of particular interest are the ten batons of a marshal or equivalent rank.

Immediately facing the main entrance to Apsley House is the Equestrian Statue in bronze. This shows the Duke on his charger Copenhagen; at the corners of the pedestal stand the uniformed figures of a Grenadier, a 42nd Royal Highlander, a 23rd Royal Welch Fusilier, and a 6th Inniskilling Dragoon.

A huge equestrian statue that had been erected adjacent to the end of Constitution Hill was removed in 1883 to Wellington Avenue, Aldershot.

Barely 200 yards from Apsley House stands the Achilles Statue in Hyde Park. This was erected in 1822, and is in the classical tradition of a hero-warrior 'cast from cannon taken in the victories at Salamanca, Vitoria, Toulouse and Waterloo'. The statue bears no resemblance to the Duke, but the inscription is worth reading closely.

Words to Remember

In the course of his long life, the Duke of Wellington evidenced a flare for the *bon mot* which would rapidly circulate and, inevitably, be altered, if only in minor detail. Much the same applies to Napoleon, some of whose remarks bear the stamp of careful preparation rather than the spontaneity that attaches to Wellington. The quotations given here relate only to Waterloo or the period close to it.

Wellington

1. (midway through the battle): 'Hard pounding this, gentlemen; let's see who will pound the longest.'

Also given as: 'Hard pounding this, gentlemen: we will try who can pound the longest.'

2. (to various formation commanders who pleaded for reinforcements): 'You must hold your ground to the last man, and all will be well.'

3. (reply to members of his entourage who had asked what his plan was so that if he were to be killed then his successor could be told what line to take): 'My plan is simply to stand my ground to the last man.'

4. (to an artillery officer, who said he had a distinct view of Napoleon and his staff, and that he could switch his guns in that direction): 'No! No! I will not allow it! It is not the business of commanders to be firing upon each other.'

5. (at a point near the end of the battle, when the infantry were in a position to charge with bayonets): 'Up, Guards, and at them!' Consulted about this very much later the Duke said that he did not think he had said precisely that, but admitted he had probably cried out 'Stand up, Guards!' as a preliminary command, to make those firing from a prone position ready to take part in the bayonet charge ordered immediately afterwards.

6. (after the battle) 'It has been a damned serious business. Blücher and I have lost 30,000 men. It has been a damned nice thing – the nearest run you ever saw!

By God! I don't think it would have done if I had not been there.'

In some quotations the phrase is: '. . . the nearest run you ever saw in your life.'

7. 'It is very true that I have said that I considered Napoleon's presence in the field equal to 40,000 men in the balance. This is a very loose way of talking; but the idea is a very different one from that his presence at a battle being equal to a reinforcement of 40,000 men.'

(This was said, to clear up some dispute, on 18th September, 1836; and the date of the original comment is not clear.)

One thing that, for sure, Wellington did *not* say was: 'Waterloo was won on the playing fields of Eton.' This comment was made by the French politician, Charles Forbes, Comte de Montalembert (1810–70) who was born in London.

Napoleon
1. (in 1813): 'You write to me that it is impossible – the word is not French.' (Alternatively, there is no such word in French.)
2. (in 1814): 'The bullet that will kill me is not yet cast.'
3. 'An army marches on its stomach.' (attributed, traditional).
4. (after 1812 retreat): 'From the sublime to the ridiculous is but a step.'
5. (at Rôchefort, when the Royal Navy prevented him escaping to America in July, 1815): 'Wherever wood can swim, there I am sure to find this flag of England.'
6. 'I have very rarely met with two-o'clock-in-the-morning courage, by which I mean unprepared courage.'

(This is the accepted English translation, but there is a finesse of difference in the actual French words which are: 'Quant au courage moral il avait trouvé fort rare (disait-il) celui de deux heures après minuit; c'est à dire le courage de l'improviste.')

Recommended Reading

Considering the importance of Wellington's defeat of Napoleon, the treatment accorded to the actual battle by eminent historians is surprisingly minimal. Thus H. A. L. Fisher in his standard work (1936 and numerous further editions) accords the battle only one paragraph of 10 lines of which seven are padding or comment. Likewise, the famous and Grand Old Man among historians, George Macaulay Trevelyan O.M., C.B.E., (1876–1962), in his standard *History of England* (1926 and numerous later editions) deals with the actual battle in no more than a handful of words. On the other hand, the work of Sir Edward Creasy (1812–78) *The Fifteen Decisive Battles of the World from Marathon to Waterloo*, published in 1851, gives an elongated account which is unhappily marred by his partiality for the Prussians and is thus not fully objective. It is not now accorded the authority once claimed for it.

Of recent works *Wellington: The Years of the Sword* by Elizabeth Longford carries ninety pages of detailed account. These are studded with footnotes which might possibly be distracting. However, because as Countess of Longford, she has family connections with Wellington's family, she has privileged access to private papers which other historians have not been able to study. Her book thus provides unique if minor insights into the battle.

An edited edition of the papers of John Wilson Croker who lived 1780–1857 is often worth consulting (*The Croker Papers* edited by Bernard Pool, published 1967), as also is Sir John Fortescue's *History of the British Army*. Colour and atmosphere come out of the pages of *The Journal of Surgeon James* who was an Army doctor at Waterloo – this is a work edited by Jane Vansittart, published 1964. Field Marshal the Viscount Montgomery of Alamein gives a much researched study of the battle in his *History of Warfare* (1968), as does Jac Weller in his *Wellington at Waterloo*.

The Irishman novelist and military fiction writer, William Hamilton Maxwell (1794–1850) wrote some amusing *Stories from Waterloo* (1829) and a serious life of Wellington. As he served in the Army, was in the Peninsular War, and fought at Waterloo, it is worth quoting his words: 'The fight at Waterloo may be easily comprehended by simply stating that for several hours it was a continued succession of attacks of the French columns on the squares; the British artillery firing upon them as they advanced and the cavalry charging when they receded.'

Caution: Do not refer to the British 'thin red line' at Waterloo. This is because the originator of the phrase was William Howard Russell (1820–1907) who, representing *The Times* newspaper in the Crimean War, was the first genuine War Correspondent. His despatch from the Crimea referred to the British redcoats as a 'thin red streak'; that being liable to misunderstanding, the expression was changed in his book *The British Expedition to the Crimea* (1877) wherein he wrote 'The Russians dash on towards that thin red line tipped with steel.' And, of course, at Waterloo there was no question of a thin red line of redcoats; the French attack was broken by the massed fire of muskets as a follow-up to merciless pounding by the guns.

Index

Allied Army, 19, 25; battle line-up, 86–9; casualties, 68; order of battle, 118–19; scale of equipment, 52; strength, 65–6; tactics, 41–51
Artillery, speed of movement, 17; types of gun, 68
Avesnes-sur-Helpe, Napoleon's start point, 32

Baker rifle, 57
Belgian troops, 102, 124, 128
Blücher, G., Feldmarschall, Prussian Commander, 28; biography, 36–7; defeat at Ligny, 101, 114; first orders to Zeiten, 29; his commanders, 78–80; into action, 94; Marshal 'Vorwarts', 116, 139; meets Wellington post-victory, 142, 164; Prussian forces, 66–7; with Wellington at Bry, 100
Bogue, Capt. Richard, his rockets, 55
Books recommended, 172
British Army (see also Allied Army), 25, 28, 43; assessment of enemy movements, 27, 28; based on Brussels, 25; dispositions and formations at Mont Saint Jean, 89–91; Dutch and Belgian comparisons, 69, 70, 71–80; divisional commanders, 71–8; equipment, 53–5; figures, 64–8; formation of a square, 47 *et seq*; secret weapons, 54 *et seq*; skirmishers, sharpshooters, 45; tactics, 46–51
Bülow, General von, 67, 120–1, 139; at Ligny, 109
Buonaparte, becomes Bonaparte, 34

Casualty figures, 146
Communications, delays, 29; fiasco, 104–8, 121, 153–4; speed of, 17
Creasy, Sir Edward, historian, 64, 173

Dutch troops, 102, 124, 128

Equipment for campaigning, 52
Erlon, Count Drouet, 102, 129; fiasco march, 104–8

French Army, corps commanders, 81–2; corps details, 161; exhortation by Napoleon, 32–3; frontier corps, 20; Guard attacks, 132 *et seq*; General Bourmont defects from, 40; options for attack on Brussels, 21; order of battle, 118–19; rate of movement, 17; strength totals, 67; tactics, 42–51; tirailleurs, dragons, cuirassiers, 45–9

Gneisenau, General von, Chief of Prussian staff, 100, 112, his dispatch, 138
Grouchy, Marshal Emanuel, 61, 67, 83, 113, 115, 121, 122, 128, 141, 155
Guard, Imperial, 57–9, 161; in battle, 113, 129, 131, 132 et seq

Hougoumont, farm-house, 120, 121, 123, 126, 129, 131, 135

Kellerman, Marshal F. C., 61, 123 et seq

La Belle Alliance, 123, 130, 131, 136, 138, 140; meeting of commanders, 142
La Haye Sainte, 123, 128, 130
Leipzig, battle of, 14, 35; Congreve rockets at, 55
Ligny, battle at, 30, 101–3, 104–8

Marshal, list of French marshals, 61–2; title and rank, 59–60
Memorials, 167–9
Müffling, General Baron von, liaison officer, 30, 39, 40, 100–1

Napoleon, at Quatre Bras, 113–14; birth, 11; character, 35; defeat at Leipzig, 14, 35; directs main battle, 132–6; escape from Elba, 15; exile and death, 165; first abdication, 15; flight in defeat, 137, 140; general biography, 33–35; his affliction, 112; his marshals, 61–2; his view of battle positions, 91–3; obiter dicta, 171; plans with Ney, 98; proclamation to Army, 35; second abdication, 142; victory at: Auerstadt, 23, Dresden, 14; Jena, 23; Marengo, 35; Wagram, 12
Ney, Marshal, M., 62, 83, 97–8, 112–13, 123, 131, 133 et seq; at Quatre Bras, 101–2; composition of massed column, 149

Orange, Prince of, at Quatre Bras, 102

Paris, Treaty of, 15
Picton, General Sir Thomas, 74, 124
Prussian forces see under Blücher; at Ligny, 108–9, 120, 122, 126, 131; commanders, 78–80

Quatre Bras cross-roads, 40, 99, 100, 107, 111, 113–14, 115, 155; Dutch and Belgian troops at, 102; French attack, 101–3; importance of, 95

Richmond, Duchess of, Ball in Brussels, 40, 99–100, 111
Rifle, Baker type, 57
Roads, state of, 17
Rockets, Congreve, 54; at Leipzig, 55; at Toulouse, 56

Sambre, River, its importance, 21, 40
'Sepoy General', 11, 150
Siborne, Capt. William, historian, 63, 64–7, 153
Soult, Marshal, defeated by Wellington at Toulouse, 15; in retreat at Waterloo, 141; in Spain, 12
'Spanish Ulcer', 13

Tactics on battlefield, 41–51
Thielman, General, 122
Tilsit, treaty terms, 23

Union Brigade, 125
Uxbridge, Lord, 144, 167

Wargame, Waterloo as, 157–160
Waterloo, battle forces involved, 63 et seq; battle line-up, 86–93; casualties, 68–70, 145–6; commanders: British, 72–8; French, 81–2; Prussian, 78–80; Imperial Guard in action, 132 et seq; opening attack, 123; order of battle, 118–19, weather, 117
Waterloo (general), battlefield model, 63; in paintings, 152–3; memorials, 167; site, 11; topography, 85–6; wargame, 157–60
Wavre, 110, 113, 114, 115, 121, 122
Weapons, secret, 54–7
Weather, 91, 111, 117; visibility factors, 162
Wellesley see under Wellington

175

Wellington, 1st Duke of; ambassador in Paris, 15; birth and early career, 11–14, 37–9; character, 39; commander of Allied forces, 16; created: Duke of Ciudad Rodrigo, 13; Duke of Wellington, 15; Earl, 13; Field Marshal, 15; Viscount, 12; Congress of Vienna, 15; defeats Soult, 15; death, 166; dispatch after the battle, 142–5; his view of battle, 86–91; in Spain, 12–15; liaison with Blücher, 30; main battle, 132–7; meets Blücher at Bry, 100; memorials 167–9; obiter dicta, 170–1; post-victory meeting with Blücher, 142; post-Waterloo career, 166; 'Sepoy General', 11, 150

Zeiten, General, 1st Prussian Corps, 29, 30, 40, 97, 98, 131, 132, 139, 163; first contacts with enemy, 29; receives French defector, 40

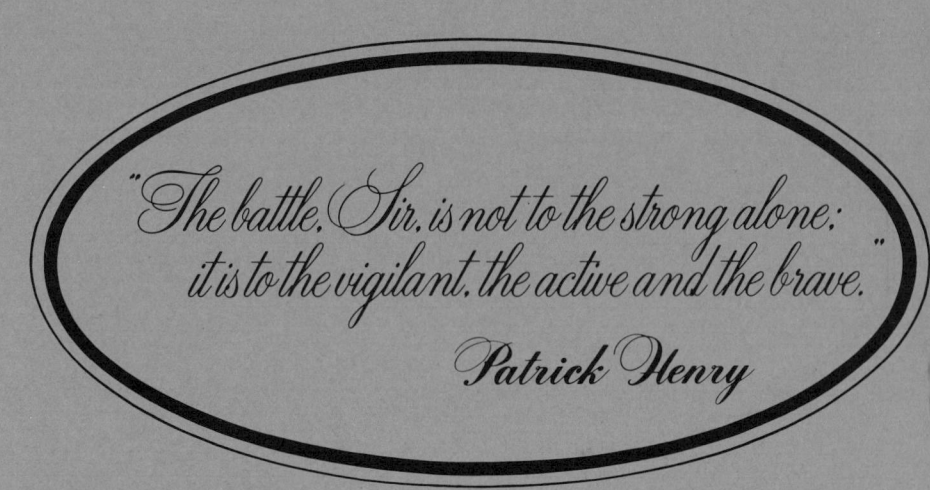

"The battle, Sir, is not to the strong alone; it is to the vigilant, the active and the brave."

Patrick Henry